The Archers

Miscellany

The Archers
Miscellany

JOANNA TOYE

To Camilla, Tony and Hattie, with love

This book is published to accompany the BBC Radio 4 series *The Archers*.
The editor of *The Archers* is Vanessa Whitburn.

10 9 8 7 6

First published in 2009 by BBC Books, an imprint of Ebury Publishing.
A Random House Group Company

Main text by Joanna Toye
Copyright © Woodlands Books Ltd, 2009

The Random House Group Limited Reg. No. 954009

Addresses for companies within the Random House Group can be found
at www.randomhouse.co.uk

A CIP catalogue record for this book is available from the British Library.

ISBN 978 1 846 07754 8

The Random House Group Limited supports The Forest Stewardship
Council (FSC), the leading international forest certification organisation.
All our titles that are printed on Greenpeace approved FSC certified paper
carry the FSC logo. Our paper procurement policy can be found at
www.rbooks.co.uk/environment

Mixed Sources
Product group from well-managed
forests and other controlled sources
www.fsc.org Cert no. TT-COC-2139
© 1996 Forest Stewardship Council

Commissioning editor: Albert DePetrillo
Project editor: Nicholas Payne
Copy-editor: Steve Tribe
Designer: O'Leary & Cooper
Maps: Draughtsman Ltd
Production: Bridget Fish

Map illustration courtesy Archers Addicts, official fan club for
BBC Radio 4's *The Archers*, www.archers-addicts.com

Printed and bound in the UK by CPI Mackays, ME5 8TD

To buy books by your favourite authors and
register for offers, visit www.rbooks.co.uk

INTRODUCTION

'You're writing *what*?' I couldn't understand why people were so surprised that there was a book to be written based on the archives of *The Archers* – to me it wasn't just an interesting idea, but an obvious one.

When I started work on the programme in 1980, *The Archers'* continuity system was typed and handwritten on thousands of index cards. They were kept in a set of miniature wooden filing drawers with domed brass handles, with labels like: 'CHARACTERS LIVING A–' (there were a lot of 'A's, obviously) or, more ominously, 'DEAD AND GONE'.

The cards had been the idea of Valerie Hodgetts, the programme's first Production Assistant back in 1951. In those days there were only two writers – not much room for confusion, you'd think. But writers, though following agreed storylines, have a nasty habit of inventing things. Writer One had patriarch Dan Archer announce that his favourite meal was steak and kidney pie; Writer Two had him favouring chicken and leek. Valerie realised that the only solution was to record not just the major events – a plane crashing into Dan's wheat or the course of Phil's romance with Grace – but the fact that Dan smoked a pipe, was Vice-President of the Cricket Club and always wore a nightshirt, never pyjamas.

This system lasted – and worked – for over forty years, until the arrival of the programme's first full-time Archivist in 1994. When Camilla Fisher applied for the job, she impressed us all not just with her encyclopaedic knowledge of the programme but also with the fact that (in what she tries to claim is a coincidence) she even got married on the same day as Shula (first time around, when Shula married Mark). Camilla gamely took on the twin tasks of not just selecting archive-relevant material from the work of the nine current scriptwriters and logging it all on computer, but the massive undertaking of computerising the continuity cards as well. That is still, understandably, an ongoing process, and for this book I spent many happy hours foraging among them, some held together with elastic bands which disintegrated at a touch, some so much handled they've fragmented at the edges into little archipelagos and have to be kept in plastic wallets. There were good moments and bad. The joy of finding, in full, Marjorie Antrobus's recipe for Yemenite pickle and the fact that there were so many recorded mentions of Nigel's jackets that they merited an entry of their own had to be set against the frustration of the 'lost years' of the Fete and Flower and Produce Show and the detective work needed to try to fill in the gaps.

In all this, Camilla generously shared her knowledge and her database and pointed me in many fruitful directions – I could not have begun, let alone completed, this book without her. The Editor of *The Archers*, Vanessa Whitburn, gave me her usual enthusiastic support throughout, and my editors at Random House, Albert DePetrillo and Nicholas Payne, nursed the book calmly through its various production stages.

This *Miscellany* – the clue is in the title – doesn't claim to be exhaustive. It's also no sociological tract, but its seemingly random details, taken together, do paint a revealing picture of a changing society and countryside in the latter twentieth and early twenty-first centuries.

Whether you're a long-time listener or a recent convert, if you're curious about the field names at Brookfield, where various characters went on their honeymoons, or who makes the best scrambled egg in the village, then this book is for you. Welcome to the complete and complex world that is Ambridge.

JOANNA TOYE
June 2009

6

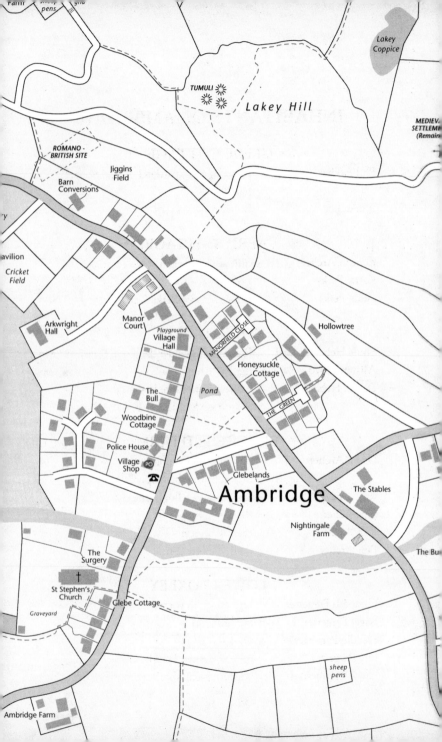

INHABITANTS OF AMBRIDGE

GLEBE COTTAGE

Phil Archer	retired farmer, patriarch of the Archer family
Jill Archer	his wife

APRIL COTTAGE

Kenton Archer	Phil and Jill's elder son
Kathy Perks	his partner
Jamie Perks	her son by Sid Perks

THE STABLES

Shula Hebden Lloyd	Phil and Jill's elder daughter, Kenton's twin
Alistair Lloyd	her husband
Daniel Hebden Lloyd	her son by her late husband, Mark Hebden, adopted by Alistair

BROOKFIELD FARM

David Archer	Phil and Jill's younger son, now running the family farm
Ruth Archer	his wife and fellow farmer
Pip Archer	their daughter
Josh Archer	their elder son
Ben Archer	their younger son

LOWER LOXLEY

Elizabeth Pargetter	Phil and Jill's younger daughter
Nigel Pargetter	her husband
Freddie Pargetter	their son
Lily Pargetter	their daughter, Freddie's twin
Lewis Carmichael	Nigel's late mother's second husband

WOODBINE COTTAGE

Christine Barford — Phil's sister, widow of George Barford

THE LODGE

Peggy Woolley — formerly married to Jack Archer,
Phil's late elder brother

Jack Woolley — her second husband

HOME FARM

Jennifer Aldridge — Peggy and Jack Archer's elder daughter

Brian Aldridge — her husband

Alice Aldridge — their daughter

Ruairi Donovan — Brian's son by his late mistress,
Siobhan Hathaway

THE DOWER HOUSE

Lilian Bellamy — Peggy and Jack Archer's younger daughter

Matt Crawford — her partner

BRIDGE FARM

Tony Archer — Peggy and Jack Archer's son

Pat Archer — his wife and fellow farmer

HONEYSUCKLE COTTAGE

Adam Macy — Jennifer's son by Paddy Redmond

Ian Craig — his partner

THE FLAT OVER THE SHOP

Helen Archer — Tony and Pat's daughter

Annette Turner — her lodger, daughter of her late partner
Greg Turner

NO 1 THE GREEN

Tom Archer — Tony and Pat's son
Brenda Tucker — his fiancée, Mike Tucker's daughter

WILLOW COTTAGE

Mike Tucker — self-employed
Vicky Tucker — his second wife

WILLOW FARM HOUSE

Roy Tucker — Mike's son
Hayley Tucker — his wife
Abbie Tucker — their daughter
Phoebe Tucker — Roy's daughter by Kate Aldridge

AMBRIDGE VIEW

Neil Carter — self-employed
Susan Carter — his wife
Christopher Carter — their son

RICKYARD COTTAGE

Emma Grundy — Neil and Susan's daughter, formerly married to Will Grundy
Ed Grundy — her partner; Will's brother
George Grundy — Emma and Will's son

CASA NUEVA

Will Grundy — Eddie and Clarrie's son; Ed's brother
Nic Hanson — his partner
Jake Hanson — Nic's son with her former partner
Mia — Nic's daughter with her former partner

KEEPER'S COTTAGE

Joe Grundy	patriarch of the Grundy family; retired tenant farmer
Eddie Grundy	his son, father of Will and Ed
Clarrie Grundy	Eddie's wife

GRANGE FARM

Oliver Sterling	co-owner of Grey Gables
Caroline Sterling	his wife and co-owner of Grey Gables

AMBRIDGE HALL

Robert Snell	self-employed/semi-retired
Lynda Snell	his wife

BLOSSOM HILL COTTAGE

Jim Lloyd	Alistair's father

THE BULL

Sid Perks	landlord
Jolene Perks	his wife; landlady
Fallon Rogers	Jolene's daughter with her previous partner

THE VICARAGE

Alan Franks	vicar
Usha Franks	his wife
Amy Franks	Alan's daughter by his late wife

THE BROOKFIELD BUNGALOW

Bert Fry	retired farm worker
Freda Fry	his wife

BORCHESTER

Jazzer McCreary	pigman and milkman
Kirsty Miller	friend of Helen Archer

BORSETSHIRE

Stephen Chalkman   former business partner of Matt Crawford
Annabelle Schrivener   lawyer

FURTHER AFIELD

Satya Khanna   Usha's aunt (Wolverhampton)
Shiv Gupta   Usha's brother (Wolverhampton)
Mabel Thompson   Alan's ex-mother-in-law (Bradford)
Heather Pritchard   Ruth's mother (Prudhoe)
Debbie Aldridge   Jennifer's daughter by her first husband
                       (Hungary)
Kate Madikane   Jennifer and Brian's daughter
                       (South Africa)

Events

- January -	- February -	- March -
Marmalade Making	Valentine's Day Shrove Tuesday Lent ————	Mothering Sunday

- April -	- May -	- June -
April Fool's Day Easter	Rogation Sunday Beating The Bounds May Bank Holidays Single Wicket Competition	Father's Day

- July -	- August -	- September -
Village Fete	Bank Holiday	Flower and Produce Show

- October -	- November -	- December -
Apple Day Harvest Festival Harvest Supper	Bonfire Night Remembrance Sunday Christmas Production Rehearsals	The Borchester Primestock Show Christmas Production

THE STORY OF APPLE DAY

Apple Day in Ambridge is celebrated on or near 21 October, usually at either Lower Loxley or on the Village Green or a less commercial event at one of the farms.

At Lower Loxley in 2006, as well as apple-themed fun, the chief attraction was 'Log To Leg' with greenwood craftsman Alec. The idea was to split a log and turn each piece into a chair leg. Usha, Nigel and Phil each managed to produce two of the required four legs in the allotted time.

At somewhere like Brookfield, Apple Day's a more casual affair, with games for the children such as bobbing for apples, apple and spoon race, and the longest piece of peel. In 2005, there was an all-apple cake stall, and Pip and Izzy made toffee apples. Lynda, armed with reference books, tried to identify apples but was stumped by a supermarket Pink Lady.

Despite being the village's Tree Warden, George Barford didn't have much more luck when he attempted the identification process at the Village Green event in 2001. He correctly identified a Russet, but baulked at the bitter Borsetshire Beauty – a cider apple – offered by a mischievous Pip. Daniel and Josh had a fun apple-bobbing, Helen ran an apple juice tent, Kathy demonstrated strudel-making and there was a competition for the longest piece of peel.

DONKEY DRAMAS

The original donkey used for the Ambridge Palm Sunday Service was called Basil. When he died, he was replaced by Benjamin, who can be rather more temperamental:

- On Palm Sunday 2003, the congregation had just begun their walk round the outside of the church behind the donkey when Lynda turned up with her llamas. The llamas, spooked by the donkey, sat down and refused to budge: so did the donkey. The congregation were forced to retrace their steps into the church to avoid the stand-off.

- There was a good turnout in 2005 for the Palm Sunday Service, this time in Darrington, Alan having supplied branches for the children to wave as well as palm crosses. Helen had already had to calm Benjamin for the procession but when the children shouted 'Hosanna', he bolted. The ecstatic children chased him till he tired himself out.

- In 2006 and 2007, Shula led Benjamin to church – both times mercifully without incident, despite Palm Sunday in 2007 falling on 1 April.

- There was a slight rapprochement between Shula and St Stephen's when she agreed to lead the donkey at the 2009 Palm Sunday service.

LOWER LOXLEY
EASTER EGG-STRAVAGANZA

In 2006, to Julia Pargetter's disgust, Lower Loxley went overboard
on its Easter event, including some eye-watering puns.

Join us this Easter Weekend for three days
of egg-straordinarily egg-citing egg-sploits!

Special attractions for the children:
- Be an Easter Eggs-plorer
- Egg-spress Yourself
- Cracking Egg-citement

And not much to Shell Out!

CELEBRATIONS ON
CORONATION DAY IN AMBRIDGE

MORNING
To be left free for people to listen to their radios
or watch television (if they had it)

AFTERNOON
Sports for the children, tea, and children
to be presented with commemorative mugs

EVENING
Supper for the old folk, dancing in the streets,
bonfire and fireworks on Lakey Hill

A POTTED HISTORY OF
THE FLOWER AND PRODUCE SHOW

Entrants vie for:

- The Lawson-Hope Cup
- The Valerie Woolley Memorial Cup
- The Nelson Gabriel Memorial Cup for Gentleman's Buttonhole

The Overall Winner is the person with the most First Prizes.

~ 1975 ~

Overall winner: Jean Harvey

1st prize ....Marrow...............................Joe Grundy

(Mrs P challenged whether it was his – it was)

~ 1976 ~

1st prize ....Marrow............................... Bert Gibbs

1st prize .... Potatoes ....Walter Gabriel

3rd prize...............................Quince Jelly.............................Jill Archer

~ 1977 ~

Overall winner: Jean Harvey

1st prize ....Lemon Curd.........................Doris Archer

(Challenged by Laura, who thought it was a jar she'd given Doris)

A prize ....Bottled gooseberries................... Betty Tucker

~ 1978 ~

Overall winner: Jean Harvey

(Disqualified as she'd used a professional gardener)

~ 1979 ~

1st prize .... Vegetables (excepting leeks)......... Freddie Danby

Highly commended....................Roses ....Doris Archer

Several prizes..Mrs Strickland,

No. 3 Glebelands

LYNDA SNELL'S
CHRISTMAS PRODUCTION 2003

The Ambridge Mystery Plays

A co-production by
Lynda Snell
and
Reverend Alan Franks

This is a peripatetic production encompassing
St Stephen's Church, The Green, Ambridge, and Brookfield Farm.

CAST LIST

HEROD	Oliver Sterling
MARY	Susan Carter
JOSEPH	Kenton Archer
SALOME, A MIDWIFE	Clarrie Grundy
SECOND MIDWIFE	Betty Tucker
ANGEL	Julia Pargetter
FIRST SHEPHERD	Bert Fry
SECOND SHEPHERD	Joe Grundy
FIRST WOMAN	Shula Hebden Lloyd
SECOND WOMAN	Kathy Perks
FIRST KING	Nigel Pargetter
SECOND KING	Neville Booth
THE DEVIL	Graham Ryder
DONKEY	Bartleby

MUSIC	Fallon Rogers
STAGE MANAGER	Neil Carter
COSTUMES	Shula Hebden Lloyd
	Caroline Pemberton
SET DESIGN	Robert Snell

As a change from a traditional panto, newly arrived vicar Alan Franks and Lynda put their heads together and decided that the Christmas show should have a more religious theme. The Mystery Plays were a peripatetic production encompassing scenes at St Stephen's, the village green and Brookfield.

HARVEST SUPPER

In the old days, when the traditional menu was boiled beef and onions with plum pudding to follow, the venue for the supper, which always starts at 7 p.m., used to be the village hall. Joe Grundy remembers that the tables used to be laid out in a horseshoe shape, with the bosses across the top and workers down the sides. Nowadays the supper is as likely to be held at The Bull Upstairs or on one of the farms.

In 1980, a £1.50 ticket bought a supper of cold ham, jacket potatoes, tomato salad and lemon meringue pie. But 1983 saw a price rise to a staggering £4 – the income was desperately needed for new guttering round the church. Happily the evening raised £300 and there was a more ambitious menu to enjoy:

Menu

Leek & Potato Soup

Pork in Red Wine Glaze
Gooseberry Sauce
Stuffed Tomatoes

Blackberry & Apple Pies
Pears in Ginger
Harvest Cake

YOU'VE NEVER HEARD OF LAMMAS-TIDE?

Penny Hassett celebrates the first wheat harvest on 1 August. They choose the biggest man in the village, dress him up as the Great Boar of Hassett and push him in a wheelbarrow down the main street. Or so Mark Hebden told an incredulous Usha on her arrival in Borsetshire...

STAR STRUCK

Richard Todd – war hero, actor... farmer? And ribbon-cutter at the Ambridge Fete in 1962? Thanks to a chance meeting at a National Dairy Farmers' Lunch, Dan managed to prevail on the movie legend to do the honours. It helped that Todd was due to attend a dispersal sale in Borsetshire around the date in question – and he turned out to be highly knowledgeable about livestock. (Dan, treating him to a pint in The Bull, learnt that he had twenty-six Jerseys with eighteen followers, as well as a flock of Border Leicester Cheviots tupped by Suffolk rams). Seventeen-year-old Jennifer, hanging round in the hope of being noticed, and disappointed by their mundane farming talk, did however manage to impress Todd with her ambition to be a nurse, and asked his advice on an important matter – should she dye her hair blonde? 'Stay as sweet as you are,' was his wise, if slightly elliptical, advice.

HALLOWEEN COSTUME CALL

- Trick or treating aged 13, William had a pretend axe in his head.
- In the same year, Brenda was the Bride of Dracula.
- Jill made Pip, aged 5, a witch's costume.
- After the 1999 children's fancy dress party at the Village Hall, the spooky backdrop was painted over for use in the Christmas Pantomime.
- Daniel was one of many Harry Potters at the Lower Loxley Children's Party in 2001.

A POTTED HISTORY OF THE FLOWER AND PRODUCE SHOW

～ 1980 ～

3rd prize.....................................Honey ....Freddie Danby

(Disappointed – his only prize)

～ 1981 ～

No Flower and Produce Show.
Ambridge held a Flower Festival instead.

～ 1982 ～

Overall winner: Pru Forrest (Accused by Walter of cheating
by using W.I. products in home-made jams section)

1st prize .... House plant .... Pru Forrest
1st prize ....Home-made wine .... Pru Forrest
A prize... Onions..........................Walter Gabriel

(Challenged by Dan, who thought they were his)

3rd prize................................. Sweet peas ....Walter Gabriel

GHOSTS OF AMBRIDGE:
SOLDIER, SOLDIER

In the early 1980s, Sid and Polly Perks couldn't understand why their 8-year-old daughter Lucy wasn't keen on her new bedroom above the pub. Claiming that it was cold, and that she heard funny noises, she simply refused to sleep there.

Walter Gabriel thought he had the answer. In the 1800s, he declared, a soldier coming home from the wars had been set upon by a gang. Escaping, he managed to crawl up to the loft above an outbuilding attached to the pub but, his strength fading, could only tap faintly on the doorway between his hiding place and the pub. No one heard him, and next morning, he was found dead.

Sid pooh-poohed the story, but when, next day, he heard an intermittent tapping in Lucy's room, he changed his mind – until he discovered the loose TV aerial tapping against the drainpipe. Lucy, however, still wouldn't use the room, so Sid asked famous Waterley Cross ghost hunter Ted Atkins to inspect it. Ted found nothing – but why let that spoil a good tale?

IT COULD BE YOU...

'Calling all beauties! As part of our annual festivities, this year we are holding a Beauty Competition!' So a flyer for the forthcoming Ambridge Fete might have read in 1977. Pat had her mind on other things (motherhood, for one) else the contest would surely have been sabotaged, but all ran smoothly, despite the judging panel including (as well as the inevitable philanthropist Jack Woolley and the bumbling Colonel Danby) not one but two notorious womanisers: Brian Aldridge, recently married to Jennifer, and Christine's first husband Paul Johnson. The girl who carried away the 'Miss Ambridge' crown (though she came from Penny Hassett) was Ellen Padbury, so Neil Carter considered himself the real winner: Ellen was his girlfriend.

CHRISTMAS LIGHTS
IN AMBRIDGE

In the first week of December, Sid turns on the Christmas lights outside The Bull. Villagers switch on theirs in sequence, then emerge on to the Green for punch and mince pies with the crowds.

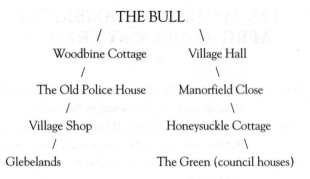

THE BULL
/ \
Woodbine Cottage   Village Hall
/   \
The Old Police House   Manorfield Close
/   \
Village Shop   Honeysuckle Cottage
/   \
Glebelands   The Green (council houses)

BE MY VALENTINE

- Mike sent Betty a card every year.
- Tom and Brenda got together on Valentine's Night.
- Tickets for Lower Loxley's Valentine's Ball in 2004 cost £125 each.
- In 2003, Roy bought Hayley a locket.
- Sid proposed to Jolene at a Valentine's Dance at the County Hotel in Borchester in 2002. Three years later, the magic still hadn't worn off: he presented her with a bunch of pink roses and a gold chain and heart engraved with 'From Sid to the love of his life'.
- Fallon and Ed once sent prank Valentines to victims including Lynda, Sid, Caroline, Oliver, Tim Hathaway and Janet Fisher.
- Usha's ex, Ashok, went over the top with a card, a bunch of lilies, a box of Underwoods Belgian chocolates, a pair of earrings AND dinner at Botticelli's.
- Every year, Bert gives Freda spring flowers that he's grown himself, but their most romantic Valentine's Day was spent on their trip to India in 2006.

TEN MEMORABLE AMBRIDGE APRIL FOOL'S DAY PRANKS

| 1986 | Nigel's friend Tim Beecham sprayed 'Elizabeth Archer wears thermal vests' on a wall in Borchester. |
| 1993 | A straight-faced Brian told Lynda that the Common Agricultural Policy was about to start paying out for domestic set-aside – she could even get a subsidy for a window box. |

1998   Spotting a vivid green lizard in the Country Park, assiduous Lynda was straight on the phone to the Borsetshire Wildlife Trust, only to learn from Eddie that the lizard (supposed breed: Aprillus Foolus) was one of Edward's pets.

1999   Eddie tricked Joe with a fake letter from MAFF instructing that all cows needed photographs on their cattle passports. He even lined up one of Snatch Foster's mates to pose as the bovine photographer.

2001   When Jennifer had trouble getting a pound coin off the pavement outside the shop, Robert spared her blushes by explaining it was an April Fool: the coin was super-glued to the surface. A gleeful Ed Grundy was taking photos of his victims.

2002   Ruth and David sat down to breakfast only to find that their boiled eggs were empty shells. Visiting grandma Heather had helped Pip and Josh recreate a favourite trick of Ruth's dad, Solly.

2003   With the help of The Bull's computers, Fallon transposed Joe's head onto the photograph of Bert (Mr April) from the recent fund-raising male nude calendar. Joe was eventually pacified by a free drink from Sid.

2004   It was Lilian's turn to be fooled when an unusually mischievous Pat and Tony sent her details of a new face cream – Lipoflora. Lilian's search for the wonder product proved mysteriously unsuccessful and it fell to Adam to put her right – and unscramble the anagram.

2005   Pip shocked her parents when she returned from friend Izzy's with blue hair, claiming it was permanent when it was in fact the 'spray-in-wash-out' variety. Heather also re-ran Solly's empty-eggshell trick with the boys.

2007   Bert sent Eddie, his rival in the Town Crier Competition, a fake letter saying that one of the heats required a cry in a foreign language – to be performed on the Green on 1 April. Eddie fell for it until Caroline pointed out that the script he was declaiming – in Italian – stated that he was an idiot and his grandfather was a goat. Eddie thought he'd been welcoming a tour party from Rome.

A POTTED HISTORY OF
THE FLOWER AND PRODUCE SHOW

～ 1983 ～
ENTRIES:

Potatoes, onions, beans	Walter Gabriel
Crystallised fruit	Pru Forrest

～ 1984 ～

A prize	Home-made wine	Freddie Danby
1st prize	Sweet peas	Dan Archer
Highly commended	Informal table decoration	Pat Archer

ENTRIES:

Tomato chutney	Pru Forrest
Piccalilli	Pru Forrest
Informal table decoration	Jennifer Aldridge

(Judge's criticism: 'Your oasis is showing.')

Sweet peas	Pru Forrest
Tomatoes	Bill Insley
Flower arranging	Jill Archer
Roses	Jennifer Aldridge

CHILDREN'S SECTION
ENTRIES:

1st prize	Animal sculpture – sweetcorn rhinoceros	Kate Aldridge
Unplaced	Animal sculpture – shark	John Archer
Unplaced	Butterfly cakes	Helen Archer

OUT OF THE FRYING PAN

In 1986, Elizabeth took part in the Penny Hassett Pancake race, coming third out of 25 entries in the 100-yard dash. The fact that it was her photo, and not the winner's, which appeared in the *Felpersham Evening Post* could have had something to do with the fact that she was wearing a French Maid's outfit.

In 1994, Shrove Tuesday was the night of vet/vicar Robin Stokes's stag night. After Mark Hebden boasted that he'd been famous for his pancakes in the Scouts, Ambridge's doctor Richard Locke seized on the idea, organising a minibus to the Malverns for a pancake-tossing competition – followed by a four-mile hike to the pub.

LYNDA SNELL'S CHRISTMAS PRODUCTION 2004

A CHRISTMAS CAROL

Though some might say this is always the case with Lynda's efforts, this show really was blighted. Kathy Perks took pity on seemingly lonely Lower Loxley chef Owen King (aka Gareth Taylor) and when Neville Booth, who was playing Mr Fezziwig, dropped out, suggested Owen for the part. She encouraged him in his performance but he misread the signals and, after a rehearsal, raped her in the village hall. A traumatised Kathy resigned from the show and Lynda had to take over her role: when Owen then failed to show up for the first night, Alan had to step in. Other cast and crew members included:

— A CHRISTMAS CAROL —

By Charles Dickens

Director: Lynda Snell • Stage Manager: Robert Snell • Musical Director: Phil Archer

CAST LIST:

Fred		Michael	
Ebenezer Scrooge	Joe Grundy	Belle	Ruth Archer
Bob Cratchit	Alistair Lloyd	Dick Wilkins	David Archer
Charity Woman 1		Dora Cratchit	Amy Franks
Charity Woman 2		Martha Cratchit	Alice Aldridge
Marley		Peter Cratchit	Christopher Carter
Ghost of Christmas Past	Kathy Perks	Belinda	
Coachman		Tiny Tim	Daniel Hebden Lloyd
Toby		Mrs. Cratchit	Susan Carter
Ned		Ghost of Christmas Yet to Come	
Scrooge as a Boy		Ignorance	
Fran (sister)	Shula Hebden Lloyd	Want	
Fezziwig	Neville Booth	Charwoman	
Young Scrooge		Laundryman	
Mrs. Fezziwig	Clarrie Grundy	Undertaker's Man	
Ghost of Christmas Present	Lilian Bellamy	Old Joe	
Cynthia		Turkey Boy	Jamie Perks
John		Poulterer	
Mary		Townspeople/Guests/Chorus	
Gilbert		Urchin	Pip Archer
Joseph			

*PLEASE NOTE: All cast members (except Scrooge, Young Scrooge, Fred, Fezziwig, Jacob Marley and Ghosts) will be expected to sing in all group numbers.

GHOST WALK
FRIDAY 31ST OCTOBER 2008, 7 P.M.

Follow a spooky route around Ambridge!
Chill to the terrible tale of Black Lawson…
Shiver in sympathy with the Little Drummer Boy…
and run from the Worm of Ambridge…

FUN FOR ALL THE FAMILY

Starting Point
The Bull
Public House

1 The Village Pond

5 Millennium Wood

4 Ambridge Hall

3 The River Am

2 The Churchyard

TICKETS £10
to include refreshments:
hot home-made soup and cider

JOE GRUNDY'S GHOST WALK
STARTING POINT: THE BULL PUBLIC HOUSE

THE LITTLE DRUMMER BOY

During the Civil War in 1642, the Earl of Essex's men stopped for victuals at The Bull following the Battle of Hassett Bridge. On the same day, they found a young drummer boy bleeding to death nearby.

Bizarrely, in the run up to the opening of the Civil War-themed restaurant at The Bull in 1995, a cannonball, supposedly a relic of the battle, fell from its secure place on a window ledge and crashed through the floorboards. A plaque in the restaurant (now merely the Family Restaurant, the Civil War theme having been short-lived) records that:

> *'On that day the 14th June, they did find a young drummer*
> *boy dying of his wounds, his arm having been shot off. It has*
> *been said that his ghost do haunt this place still.'*

To this day, the ghostly drummer boy can reputedly be heard on occasion tapping on the wall, seeking help.

FANCY DRESS

The Friends of *Borchester General Hospital* invite you to a *Fancy Dress Ball* to be held at the

County Hotel, Borchester,

on

19th November 1983 at 7.30 for 8 p.m.

Carriages at midnight.
Prize for best costume.
Raffle prizes:
Bottle of champagne; hot air balloon flight;
dinner for two at Grey Gables Country House Hotel, Ambridge.

Here's how the residents of Ambridge were inspired to dress:

Brian – The Scarlet Pimpernel
Jennifer – Mme de Pompadour
Tony – Superman
Pat – Little Bo-Peep
Shula – Harem Girl
Nigel – Gorilla
Mark Hebden – Highwayman
Sarah Locke (Mark's then fiancée) – The Wicked Lady

FIVE CLUBS AND SOCIETIES FROM AMBRIDGE'S EARLY YEARS

THE GREY SQUIRREL CLUB

Non-PC as it now sounds, despite the predations of greys into the native red squirrel population, the Ambridge branch was formed by Tom Forrest in February 1953 to run Saturday-morning shoots with cartridges obtained through the County Agricultural Committee.

THE AERO CLUB

This was started up in 1957 on the site of the old aerodrome… and flew off into the sunset. It was never heard of again.

THE HOME SAFETY COMMITTEE

Set up by indefatigable Ambridge domestic Mrs Scroby, this met one night a week in the 1950s. Interested parties included Doris Archer, John Tregorran, Carol Grey and Mrs Fairbrother. Though it was Jack Archer's carelessness around the pub which had got Mrs Scroby's back up in the first place, Jack never attended.

THE HOLIDAY CLUB

This was formed in 1973. Villagers saved weekly for either their own family holidays or for organised trips out. Perhaps something the credit crunch could see revived?

THE AMBRIDGE SCOUT TROOP

With Phil as leader, this went from strength to strength in the 1970s, though Jill thought he had taken on too much, proved in her opinion when he crashed his car and was breathalysed. Phil, however, wouldn't listen: Jack Woolley gave him a bugle for ceremonial occasions and he enrolled on a Scout Leaders' training course.

JOE GRUNDY'S GHOST WALK
STOP NUMBER ONE: THE VILLAGE POND

POOR FLORRIE HOSKINS

Florrie Hoskins' jawbone was found in the village pond in 1990, having lain there for eighty-five years. Alone, pregnant and despairing, she'd drowned herself on All Hallow's Eve, 1905. When she discovered that Florrie had once lived in her cottage, village postmistress Martha Woodford became troubled by Florrie's fate and was convinced that Florrie had returned to haunt her former home since her remains had been disturbed. In a bid to quiet Florrie's troubled spirit, she scattered rose petals on the pond.

A POTTED HISTORY OF
THE FLOWER AND PRODUCE SHOW

~ 1985 ~

Overall winner: Pru Forrest (A record 15 first prizes)

1st prize	Jam (rose petal)	Pru Forrest
2nd prize	Jam (rhubarb and ginger)	Pru Forrest
3rd prize	Jam	Mrs P
1st prize	Bottled gooseberries	Marjorie Antrobus

TOM'S TRAUMA

The bald facts conceal the true sacrifice: the Flower and Produce Show of 1985 almost blew apart one of Ambridge's happiest marriages. In her quest for a record number of first prizes, Pru Forrest was so busy baking and bottling that she neglected to feed husband Tom. Village gossips had him reduced to stealing blobs of jam left around the kitchen to check for setting points only to be harangued for doing so. Driven to the pub for sustenance, he had to endure the sneers of Joe and Eddie, who told him he could do with losing a bit of weight – they'd long ago christened him 'Fatman Forrest'.

～ 1986 ～

Winner of the Valerie Woolley Memorial Cup: Pru Forrest

～ 1987 ～

Winner of the Valerie Woolley Memorial Cup: Pru Forrest

～ 1988 ～

No Flower and Produce Show.
Ambridge held a Ploughing Contest instead.

～ 1989 ～

No Flower and Produce Show.
Ambridge held a Giant Car Boot Sale instead.

LENT TORMENT

Lent often starts with a bet:

- The Hebden Lloyds started the new Millennium the hard way, Shula betting Alistair he couldn't give up alcohol. He retaliated by betting her she couldn't give up chocolate. Their biggest test was a box of liqueur chocolates from a grateful patient: after Alistair suggested he bite off the ends and she suck out the middles, Shula gave them to Jill for safe-keeping, intending to claim them back. Not realising this, Jill and Jennifer demolished them at a sitting.

❧ In 2003, appropriately, David challenged Alistair to the 'Three Peaks Challenge': Ben Nevis, Scafell Pike and Snowdon in twenty-four hours. This was scaled down to a more realistic (and local) target: Lakey Hill, Heydon Berrow and the Church Tower. The whole village got involved and, to complicate things, had to complete the course in Fancy Dress. Lynda got stuck on the tower stairs and had to be cut out of her costume – a Fabergé egg.

❧ In 2007, Eddie rashly bet Lilian she couldn't give up alcohol: nor could he, she retorted. The fight was on. Each would give the Church Urban Fund £50 if they failed and the other made it. Neither did, having jointly schemed to keep drinking. When Clarrie found out, she made Eddie unblock the church toilet. Matt, usually so astute, never discovered the truth – and took Lilian on a shopping trip to New York as a reward. Eddie's sponsors included Fat Paul (£20) and Mr Pullen, who gave £2 more than he'd pledged. Stephen Chalkman sponsored Lilian for £5 per day, doubled if she went the full forty days (£400), while Brian topped this by offering her £500 to go the distance. Between them, Eddie and Lilian collected well over a thousand pounds.

'I SEE A TALL, DARK, HANDSOME STRANGER...'

Fortune Tellers at the Ambridge fete have included:

- Martha Woodford
- Usha
- Lynda Snell
- Laura Archer

In the 1970s fortune tellers seemed much more exotic: Madame Algaria in 1975 and Madame Selina in 1977. The truth was more prosaic: the same person from Penny Hassett told villagers' fortunes every year, under a different name.

HARVEST SUPPER: EAT

- In 1992, Caroline helped her then boyfriend, vet and part-time vicar Robin Stokes, to plan a 'Rich Man, Poor Man' theme to highlight global poverty. A third of the Ambridge guests would get a full meal; the rest, rice and water. As luck – and, Joe would say, life – would have it, he got the Poor Man's meal and Brian the Rich Man's.
- Joe's bad luck continued the next year. Arriving late, he missed out on Jill's delicious casseroles and had to have Lynda's vegetarian alternative.
- It was Jennifer's turn to feel aggrieved in 1997. The Harvest Supper toured the four parishes, with a course in each. Pudding in Ambridge was her responsibility, but no-one had room.

- ❦ The following year, a similar catastrophe: vicar Janet Fisher had already forced down a full Harvest Supper in Darrington when she was faced with fruit pie in Ambridge. She hid it under the lectern at St Stephen's where it was later discovered by a bemused parishioner.
- ❦ The menu caused further problems the first time the theme was 'Local Produce': even the doughty W.I. found their mettle tested. In the end the revellers enjoyed a baron of beef from Oliver and Hassett Hills lamb washed down with Grundy cider.

AMBRIDGE WOMEN'S INSTITUTE

The Ambridge W.I. was founded in 1927 and meets in the evenings. Mrs Lawson-Hope, the Squire's wife, was President for many years, as was Doris Archer, who also had the honour of representing Ambridge at a Buckingham Palace Garden Party. Delegates to the Albert Hall A.G.M. have included Carol Tregorran, Mary Pound, Betty Tucker and Marjorie Antrobus, who was a long-standing member of Waterley Cross W.I. before her move to Ambridge.

In 1966, Ambridge was a runner-up for the county prize in a national W.I. competition for a scrapbook recording village history, while in 1969 they got to the regional finals of a choral competition with 'The Brilliant and The Dark'.

Outings have included a trip to the Norfolk lavender fields, a Barry Manilow concert and *As You Like It* (with Darrington W.I.).

Ambridge W.I. has campaigned for local food, reduced food miles, improved school meals and better rural housing, and against the sale and use of aerosols and the closure of rural Post Offices. Jennifer was Ambridge W.I.'s representative at a National Energy Conference as long ago as 1978.

TEN THINGS TO REMEMBER ABOUT CHRISTMAS
≈❧

- ❧ Robert likes to see his daughters; Lynda finds Leonie difficult.
- ❧ Debbie hates Christmas shopping.
- ❧ The Bridge Farm Archers decorate their tree together.
- ❧ Hayley and Roy visit her family in Birmingham.
- ❧ Bert and Freda visit their son Trevor and family (wife Barbara, daughter Amy) or have them to stay.
- ❧ The Carters visit Ivy and Bert Horrobin (Susan's parents) some time on Christmas Day.
- ❧ Jamie normally spends Christmas Day with his mum and Boxing Day with his dad.
- ❧ Freda likes to get her Christmas decorations up early: she loves Christmas.
- ❧ Robert puts up the Snells' decorations on Advent Sunday and not a day before.
- ❧ Oliver doesn't do Christmas shopping. He leaves all that sort of thing to Caroline.

A SIGN OF THE TIMES
〜〜〜

Eddie had his first (official) pint at The Dirty Duck in Borchester. Now spruced up, it's made the most of its riverside location by rechristening itself The Old Corn Mill.

A POTTED HISTORY OF
THE FLOWER AND PRODUCE SHOW

～ 1990 ～

Rivalry began between the Frys and the Forrests. Tom Forrest remained convinced to his dying day that if only Jack Woolley, rather than Cameron Fraser, had judged the tomatoes, the result could have been so, so different…

Prizes
Overall winner: Freda Fry

Highly Commended	Dahlias	Jean Harvey
A prize	Radishes	Mrs Bagshawe
1st prize	Jam (rhubarb and ginger)	Freda Fry
2nd prize	Jam	Pru Forrest
3rd prize	Jam (blackberry)	Peggy Archer
1st prize	Blackberry wine	Pru Forrest
1st prize	Lemon cheese	Pru Forrest
1st prize	Tomatoes	Freda Fry
2nd prize	Tomatoes	Pru Forrest

Entries:

Fruit cake	Pru Forrest
Dahlias	Pru Forrest
Marrow	Tom Forrest

Children's Section

Potato sculpture	William Grundy

BAD BOY WILLIAM

William hasn't always been the Goody Two-Shoes Grundy. Clarrie was abashed when in 1990 she prodded her 8-year-old prodigy to recite the poem he'd composed for the Children's 'Junior Creative' Section of the Flower and Produce Show. She'd foolishly not vetted the verse which ran:

> *'There was a young boy from Brum*
> *Who never felt nothing but glum*
> *A friend came to his aid*
> *By trying to persuade*
> *His sister to show him her bum.'*

Unfortunately, Clarrie's chosen audience was Peggy. William received a hefty clout and an even more severe punishment: he was forced to enter the 'Potato Sculpture' section instead.

JOE GRUNDY'S GHOST WALK
STOP NUMBER TWO: THE CHURCHYARD

'BLACK' LAWSON

There can't be many people who make Matt Crawford look like an upstanding citizen, but John or 'Black' Lawson comes pretty close. His catalogue of crimes towards the end of the seventeenth century included mistreating his wife, whipping his dogs, drinking to excess and exploiting his poor tenant farmers.

One night, he was returning from the hunt when two stray hounds startled his horse. Swearing and cursing, he drove his terrified mount across Heydon Berrow. The horse fell, breaking its neck – and Lawson's.

Depending on which variant of the story you believe, his ghost appears every year on All Soul's Day or on Lady Day in March (a quarter day for rent collection).

LYNDA SNELL'S CHRISTMAS PRODUCTION 2005

The Spirit of Christmas

Conceived by Julia Pargetter-Carmichael
Produced by Lynda Snell

Please note that, following the recent sad deaths of
Mrs Pargetter-Carmichael and Mrs Betty Tucker,
a retiring collection will be held in aid of
Heart and Stroke Charities

Open-mic comedy
KENTON ARCHER

Comic song - "A New Vicar's First Christmas"
REV ALAN FRANKS

It's Magic!
EDGAR TITCOMBE assisted by EILEEN PUGSLEY

Let's Dance!
PIP ARCHER and IZZY BLAKE

Recitation - "Christmas Day in the Workhouse"
JOE GRUNDY

"Frosty the Snowman"
VILLAGE CHILDREN led by HAYLEY TUCKER

Musical Spoons
DEREK FLETCHER

The Twelve Days of Christmas
LYNDA SNELL

Rudolph the Red-Nosed Reindeer
ALAN AND AMY FRANKS

Props - USHA GUPTA
Lighting and Set design - ROBERT SNELL, NEIL CARTER

When the newly married Julia Pargetter-Carmichael beat her to the coveted Christmas hall booking and started rehearsals for a festive revue, Lynda was outraged, but there was little she could do. When Julia died suddenly in November, however, Lynda had to step into the breach, though not in the circumstances she would have wished.

TOP THREE TEAM NAMES

- The Grundys' car 'Death Wish' may have had spiked wheels but it was no match for Alice's 'Pegasus' in the remote-controlled car race at the Ambridge fete in 2001 when, in an early demonstration of her technical know-how, Alice stormed away with the prize. With their groan-inducing 'TEAM CAR-TER' T-shirts, perhaps the Carters deserved to come nowhere…

- At the wartime-themed fete in 2005, Kathy and Hayley, then working together at Lower Loxley, entered the assault course as 'Mum's Army' but Alan and Tom's hopes as part of the 'Dambusters' were blitzed when Tom fell off the plank into the pond, leaving Usha and Ruth to emerge the victors as 'The Land Girls'.

- When the discovery of a Civil War grave made a seventeenth-century theme for the 2008 fete a no-brainer, no fancy names were needed, though Kenton was quick to leap into fancy dress as Captain of the Cavaliers' Tug of War Team. (This was a promotion from two years previously: at the Vegetable Olympics he was a mere 'Captain Vegetable'.) The Roundhead team was headed by Mike Tucker, whose cohorts Ed and Jazzer mocked Kenton's luxuriant wig as 'Russell Brand on a bad hair day'.

TALES FROM MOTHERING SUNDAY

- Although they're not close, Caroline goes to see her mother who is frail and in a nursing home.
- In 2006, Ruth spent Mothering Sunday milking the cows (David had hurt his shoulder).
- Pip and Phil once entertained Ruth and Jill with a piano duet for Mothering Sunday.
- After the revelation of his affair with Siobhan, Brian lurked in the lambing shed on the day.
- In 2004, David gave Jill a bottle of perfume and some freesias.
- Phoebe phones Kate on Mothering Sunday.
- In 2008, Adam gave Jennifer an antique perfume bottle which he and Ian had found at an antique fair. She also had a card and present from Ruairi.
- On the first Mothering Sunday after their marriage, Daniel and Alistair took Shula for a rather chilly picnic beside the Am. Daniel chose the food: jelly beans, chocolate buttons and cola. Luckily Alistair had brought hot consommé as well.

ROYAL WEDDING

Like the rest of the country, Ambridge pulled out all the stops in 1981 for the wedding of Prince Charles and Lady Diana Spencer. The Organising Committee included Polly Perks, Tom Forrest and Jennifer Aldridge, and a full day of fun was laid on, including tea and games on the village green for forty-two children under the age of 15. Each child was given a commemorative coin and a mug filled with sweets, while Joe provided hessian sacks for the sack race. The over-15s, meanwhile, had a disco in the village hall. The pig which Phil Archer donated for the evening barbecue at The Bull weighed 180lbs before slaughter, 120 lbs after and the resulting pork rolls cost 35 pence each.

A POTTED HISTORY OF THE FLOWER AND PRODUCE SHOW

∼ 1991 ∼

Overall Winner: Pru Forrest
(most of the villagers, including Freda Fry, deliberately
pulled out of classes so that Pru, who'd had a stroke, could claim the
title with produce she'd made earlier in the year.)

∼ 1992 ∼

No Flower and Produce Show.
Ambridge participated in the Open Gardens Scheme instead.

∼ 1993 ∼

Overall Winners: Tom Forrest and Bert Fry
(fittingly, given the above)

∼ 1994 ∼

Henri Touvier, the visiting French Mayor of Meyruelle,
judged the Onion Section and caused a storm when
he favoured young William over veteran Tom.

1st prize	Onions	William Grundy
2nd prize	Onions	Tom Forrest
Highly Commended		Mr Watson

Mike Tucker was Highly Commended in several sections,
but there was fuss about him being a 'commercial grower'.

~ **1995** ~

1st prize	Marrow	Lynda Snell
2nd prize	Marrow	Tom Forrest

(who'd given Lynda the successful seed)

1st prize	Onions	Usha Gupta
2nd prize	Onions	Tom Forrest
2nd prize	Chutney	Usha Gupta

GHOSTS OF AMBRIDGE:
THE ROUNDHEAD SOLDIER

In 1988, Brookfield sold off an outlying barn for conversion into housing. When Tom Forrest saw a troubling shadow there one evening, Lynda's researches revealed yet another wounded Civil War soldier – a Roundhead this time – who'd taken refuge and died in a cottage formerly on the site. From time to time, strange phenomena had been recorded, the last being during the Second World War when a bomb was jettisoned nearby. Lynda concluded that the building work had once again disturbed the site and the haunting had returned.

Shortly afterwards, fire gutted the entire top floor of the barn. While most blamed vandals, Lynda was convinced the ghost had caused the blaze and, strange but true, next day, Tom Forrest found a coin dating from the Civil War in the ruins. The fire inspector's investigation blamed an electrical fault, but try telling Lynda that.

EYES ON THE PRIZE

For a religious festival, Easter brings out a very competitive streak in Ambridge:

When Sid held an Easter Egg hunt at The Bull in 1990, the clues were so obscure that the eggs were only found after the slugs had been at them. Sid moaned about the mess.

In 1995, with Guy Pemberton as judge, William won the Painted Egg competition which meant that the following year, along with the Bishop, he judged the Best Simnel Cake (won by Phil Archer).

At The Bull in 1998, Susan Carter won the Easter Bonnet competition, wearing a hat made by 9-year-old Christopher. The prize was a family meal voucher; Neil asked if they could use it for the meal they'd just had.

When Grey Gables chef Jean-Paul judged the Simnel Cake competition in 1999, the joint winners were Jill Archer and Clarrie Grundy. Entry fee was £1; as eighteen cakes were entered, this meant a prize pot of £18. Clarrie was only expecting £9 but, knowing things were tight for the Grundys, Jill insisted she should have it all.

In 2004, the W.I. Simnel Cake competition judging fell to Jean-Paul's replacement Ian Craig. Lynda entered an authentic seventeenth-century recipe which featured an unbreakable crust, but as Ian couldn't cut it, it was disqualified. Kathy won; Phil came second.

Lynda did triumph, though, in the Easter Bonnet competition the same year. Judge Alan Franks was bowled over by her bonnet with its Carmen Miranda theme and Latin American musical accompaniment.

JOE GRUNDY'S GHOST WALK
STOP NUMBER THREE: THE RIVER AM

THE HOB HOUND

Forget the Hound of the Baskervilles: the Borsetshire Hob Hound is truly red in tooth and claw. The fearsome beast, with its red eyes and poisonous breath, is said to have frightened to death a poor village woman in the winter of 1844. Though the death occurred on the Borchester Turnpike, Joe has, quite naturally, appropriated the story for Ambridge.

MIXED MESSAGES

When Mrs Antrobus press-ganged her into addressing the W.I. on the theme of 'A Taste of India', Usha, who hadn't long arrived in Ambridge, duly attended and explained several aspects of Asian culture, such as Bhangra dancing and how to tie a sari. Having expected a cookery demonstration, the audience, though fascinated, were slightly disappointed – until Usha produced a range of Indian snacks. So delicious were they that Mrs A. suggested a cookery demo next time – little knowing that Usha was no cook and the food was courtesy of a takeaway in Birmingham's 'Balti Triangle'.

THE AMBRIDGE VILLAGE FETE

The Ambridge fete with its traditional stalls and sideshows was frequently enlivened in the early years by guest appearances by celebrities who performed ribbon-cutting duties:

1952	28 June	Opened by popular radio personality Gilbert Harding
1957	5 July	Opened by Humphrey Lyttleton.
1962	28 July	Opened by actor and war hero Richard Todd.

A POTTED HISTORY OF THE FLOWER AND PRODUCE SHOW

～ 1996 ～

1st prize	Jam	Jill Archer
2nd prize	Onions	Tom Forrest
3rd prize	Onions	Bert Fry
1st prize	Potatoes	Tom Forrest
3rd prize	Potatoes	Bert Fry
1st prize	Rudbeckias	Usha Gupta
2nd prize	Rudbeckias	Lynda Snell
3rd prize	Rudbeckias	Len Webster
2nd prize	Chrysanthemums	Lynda Snell

～ 1997 ～

Highly commended	Jam (blackberry)	Hayley Jordan
1st prize	Marrow	Tom Forrest

(despite Hayley having turned his best one into jam)

～ 1998 ～

No Flower and Produce Show. In a year of major fundraising in Ambridge, the villagers were busy with a Fashion Show and 'Bring Your Dogs' weekend at Grey Gables and a Sponsored Bike Ride.

～ 1999 ～

CHILDREN'S SECTION

1st prize	Longest runner bean	Pip Archer

AMBRIDGE CHRISTMAS PARTIES

- Staff at Bridge Farm/Ambridge Organics
- Staff at Grange Farm
- Staff at Grey Gables
- Staff at Lower Loxley
- Tenants at The Business Units
- Borchester Land

FREQUENT HOSTS

- Jennifer and Brian
- Matt and Lilian
- The Chalkmans
- The Streatfields
- The Snells

HALLOWEEN BRINGS OUT THE KID IN KENTON

Kenton's game of 'Murder' went horribly wrong in 2002 when he spilt fake blood over one of Lower Loxley's antique silk carpets. Undeterred, the following year he was to be seen sporting *Rocky Horror Show* fishnets and high heels to host a Gothic Horror Night at Jaxx café. In 2004, his daughter Meriel was visiting from New Zealand, and Kenton took her and Daniel trick or treating, including spooking Derek Fletcher. In 2007, the fun switched back to Jaxx, where the 'specials' on the menu had ghostly names and all the staff dressed up, with Kenton presiding as Count Dracula. The fun didn't end there for Kathy and Jamie who, courtesy of Kenton, enjoyed a takeaway and *Ghostbusters* DVD back at April Cottage.

35 FETE-FUL YEARS OF FUN AND FUNDRAISING!

1974	22 July	Ladies' Victorian Cricket Match vs the Ambridge Cricket team interrupted by a thunderstorm
1975	26 July	Police Motorcycle display; Steam Engine Race; Hollerton Town Band
1976	31 July	Pony Club display; Guess Your Weight; Talent Competition
1977	30 July	Ambridge Beauty Queen won by Ellen Padbury, Neil Carter's then girlfriend
1978	5 August	Children's painting competition won by Lucy Perks
1979	28 July	Guess the Weight of the Calf; Tug of War won by Penny Hassett
1980	19 July	Hollerton Town Band; Fortune teller
1981	15 August	Disco in the evening at the Village Hall
1982	17 July	Stalls and a marquee
1983	16 July	Beautiful Baby won by William; Bowling for a Pig won by Susan Horrobin (now Carter)
1984	7 July	200 Yard Dash won by Pat; Caroline did Face Painting
1985	6 July	Dog Show; Playgroup Fancy Dress: Roy Tucker had buckskins made out of brown paper and Kate Aldridge went as Superwoman
1986	18 July	Wet sponge stall; Tombola; 'Guess The Smell'
1987	3 August	Welly Wanging; Magical Mystery Tour
1988	1 August	Rain. Stall Holders in costume. Mr Pullen occupied the Portaloo for most of the afternoon
1989	29 May	No fete: Spring Festival instead
1990	19 August	Bonny Baby Competition won by Christopher Carter (boys) and Kylie Richards (girls); Raft Race
1991	24 August	Clarrie won the Town Crier Competition

1992	3 August	Edgeley Morris Dancers
1993	31 July	Human Fruit Machine
1994	29 July	Rain; Usha told Fortunes
1995	14 July	Duck Race
1996	21 June	Summer Festival: Talent Contest
1997	25 June	Felpersham Flyers did a fly-past; Pets' Karaoke
1998	26 July	Gut barging; Lynda told Fortunes
1999	6 August	Ambridge in the Year 1000; stallholders in costume; Boat Race; Great Thor Axe Throwing
2000	20 August	Spile-troshing; Sheep race; Five-A-Side Football
2001	18 August	Arm wrestling: Mike beats Eddie; Jolene beats Mike; Model car race; 'Dunk The Professional' – (vicar) Janet, (doctor) Tim and (solicitor) Usha
2002	1 August	Free-for-all football match through village. Eddie and Fat Paul's Disco Diggers Display
2003	20 July	Guess the Weight of the Llama; Wife-Carrying Contest won by Helen and Greg, prize presented by new vicar Alan
2004	18 July	Bushtucker Trials; Greasy Pole; Duck Race won by Matt
2005	10 July	War-time theme. Assault course; Jitterbug lessons and display by Mike and Betty; Nigel, Kenton and David as the Andrews Sisters
2006	23 July	Vegetable Olympics – carrot skittles, swede shot-put, parsnip javelin, leek tossing; Maypole Dance
2007	22 July	Traditional Fete – coconut shy, tractor pull, hoopla, face painting, Hollerton Silver band, Soak The Vicar, Sock the Dog, Guess the Weight, Darts
2008	20 July	Civil War Theme; Tug of War won by Kenton's team; Susan's Swap Club Stall
2009	12 July	Fete opened by Antony Gormley, inspiration for the Ambridge Plinth; Mobile belfry

LYNDA SNELL'S
CHRISTMAS PRODUCTION 2006

A *Lynda Snell* Production:

Snow White
&
the Seven
(Slightly Taller Than Average)
Dwarves

Starring

Snow White	Alice Aldridge
The Prince	Fallon Rogers

The Dwarves:

Lofty	Joe Grundy
Lanky	Bert Fry
Average	Kenton Archer
Shorty	Edgar Titcombe
Teeny	Christopher Carter
Weeny	Jazzer McCreary
Titch	Daniel Hebden Lloyd
Wicked Queen	Jill Archer
The Mirror	Lilian Bellamy
Huntsman	Alistair Lloyd
Lady at Court	Venetia Streatfield
Backstage Manager	Neil Carter
Music	Valda Phelps
Costumes	Caroline Pemberton
Prompt	Brian Aldridge
Make-up	Toyah Harvey

In 2006, Lynda was determined to get things under way early, but persuading people to take part was, as ever, a thankless task, not helped by the fact that – with the exception of Daniel – the dwarves spent the whole time bickering about who was taller than whom. Jill was surprisingly scary as the Wicked Queen and Lilian, aided by the odd forbidden on-stage cigarette, an effective Mirror.

HARD DONE BY?

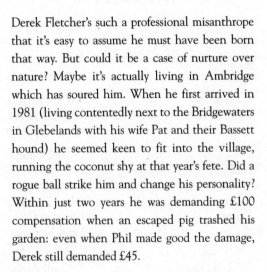

Derek Fletcher's such a professional misanthrope that it's easy to assume he must have been born that way. But could it be a case of nurture over nature? Maybe it's actually living in Ambridge which has soured him. When he first arrived in 1981 (living contentedly next to the Bridgewaters in Glebelands with his wife Pat and their Bassett hound) he seemed keen to fit into the village, running the coconut shy at that year's fete. Did a rogue ball strike him and change his personality? Within just two years he was demanding £100 compensation when an escaped pig trashed his garden: even when Phil made good the damage, Derek still demanded £45.

HARVEST SUPPER: GREET

🦊 The food was of less concern in 1999 than who would, or could, attend: David, who was to be a witness, couldn't be in the same room as Tom, who was on trial for the Home Farm GM crop trashing.

🌾 There was an emotional moment in 2000, the year of Ruth's mastectomy, when the supper was in aid of cancer charities as well as parish funds. The raffle raised over £150 and Ruth, drawing the tickets, impulsively made a speech thanking the village.

🌾 Harvest Supper 2002 was a chance for Brian to repair things with Tony after he'd stepped in as Tom's 'business angel', waxing lyrical about the potato salad made with Bridge Farm spuds.

🌾 Alan's literal interpretation of the parable of the talents – he gave interested parishioners £5 each to invest for the good of the church – culminated at the Harvest Supper in 2006. The Grundys had come good: Joe had spent his fiver on bagging up Bartleby's manure for sale and Eddie's remaining whistling gnomes were auctioned off.

🌾 It was at the Harvest Supper-cum-Barn Dance in 2007 that Fallon dragged a reluctant Ed into a do-si-do and he began to look on her as more than just a mate…

A POTTED HISTORY OF THE FLOWER AND PRODUCE SHOW

～ 2000 ～

Derek Fletcher now enters the fray

2nd prize	Jam (rhubarb)	Freda Fry
Highly Commended	Chutney	Freda Fry
1st prize	Onions	Mike Tucker

(after dispute between George and Bert over which of the two of them would win)

1st prize	Runner beans	Jill Archer
2nd prize	Runner beans	Bert Fry
3rd prize	Runner beans	Derek Fletcher
Highly commended	Rudbeckias	Usha Gupta

(Bert didn't win any first prizes)

CHILDREN'S SECTION

1st prize	Miniature garden	Pip Archer
3rd prize	Drawing (of water vole)	Daniel Hebden

∼ 2001 ∼

More categories than ever; some new categories including
Gentleman's Buttonhole and for the children, Filling a Matchbox,
Dressing a Scarecrow and Making a Model out of Rubbish

1st prize	Men Only Victoria Sponge	Christopher Carter
Unplaced	Men Only Victoria Sponge	Joe Grundy
Unplaced	Men Only Victoria Sponge	Bert Fry
1st prize	Gladioli	Bert Fry
1st prize	Beetroot	Bert Fry
1st prize	Onions	George Barford
1st prize	Shallots	George Barford

ENTRIES:

Beans	Bert Fry
Carrots	Bert Fry
Onions	Bert Fry
Courgettes	George Barford

JOE'S SECRET

Joe Grundy has a hot tip for growing kidney beans:
line the bean trench with sheep dags
(the soiled and matted wool from around a sheep's backside).

ST STEPHEN'S CHURCH, AMBRIDGE

LENT APPEAL 2004 IN AID OF COLOMBIAN HOMELESS PROMISES AUCTION

Lots to Include

(Item)	(Donated by)
Freezer pack of Hassett Hills Lamb	David and Ruth Archer
Afternoon of Llama Trekking	Lynda Snell
Falconry Day at Lower Loxley	Nigel and Elizabeth Pargetter
An afternoon's ironing	Alice Aldridge and Amy Franks
A Golf Lesson with Grey Gables Pro	Jack Woolley
A Meal Cooked In Your Own Home	Ian Craig
Casino night in the company of Mrs Lilian Bellamy	Brian Aldridge
3 Ballroom Dancing Lessons	Mike and Betty Tucker
A Digger Bucketful of Manure	Joe and Eddie Grundy

JOE GRUNDY'S GHOST WALK
STOP NUMBER FOUR: AMBRIDGE HALL

JOHN BRIAR AND THE SQUIRE

John Briar was a travelling tinker who died as a result of the heartlessness of the local squire. According to Joe, his great-great-great-great aunt was a kitchen maid to Squire Dyke, and John Briar was sweet on her.

Jennifer uncovered a scandalous story from the eighteenth century about one of the Lawson-Hopes (later to become local bigwigs the Lawson-Hopes) and a merchant called John Briand. She was convinced it was the root of Joe's (inaccurate) John Briar story. When Alan, Phil and Jill investigated further in the church archive, foolishly choosing to do this on a wild Halloween night itself, they found out that Richard Lawson-Hope had falsely accused John Briand of theft and had him hanged so that Richard could marry the widow. Mysteriously, Richard himself was registered dead just two weeks later. As a storm raged round the church, they read that Jean Briand manufactured slipware which was marked with the family stamp of a fox. The church door blew open, the lights went out and Phil saw the flashing eyes of a fox reflected in the light of his torch.

A STRAIGHT FURROW: BORSETSHIRE PLOUGHING MATCHES

Bert uses a restored vintage Massey Ferguson 165 diesel, while his rival Jimmy Prentice uses a Fordson. They compete in the South Borsetshire Ploughing Cup; there is a shield for the runner-up. The judges include Kenny Fairclough and Andy Kirkham.

Apart from the notorious Jimmy, Bert's closest Ploughing Match rivals in the Vintage Class are John Bolstrom and Vernon Giddins. In the Reversible Ploughing Competition for Modern Tractors in which Bert competed in 2001, his challengers were John Davies from Little Croxley and Simon Skelding from Penny Hassett.

Ploughing Matches have taken place at Netherbourne, Edgeley, Brampton Green, Beckwell and at Steven Watson's farm.

The specialist tractor engineer in Felpersham, Dennis Wiggins, used to work for Borsetshire Agricultural.

Past contestants in Ploughing Matches have included:

- Dan Archer
- Walter Gabriel
- Ned Larkin
- Bert Gibbs

- John Archer
- Ruth Archer
- Debbie Aldridge
- Brian Aldridge
- Joe Grundy
- Alf Grundy

ODE ON A FORDSON

Though he now competes on a Massey, Bert once composed a poem in praise of a Fordson tractor.

CONTRIBUTIONS
TO THE AMBRIDGE FETE
BOTTLE STALL, 1982

Elderflower wine and raspberry cordial	Tom and Pru Forrest
2 bottles food colouring	Jethro Larkin
A gallon of Kingston Black cider	Joe Grundy (in error)

A POTTED HISTORY OF
THE FLOWER AND PRODUCE SHOW

2002

1st prize	Marrow	Bert Fry
1st prize	Parsnips	Bert Fry
1st prize	Beetroot	Bert Fry
3rd prize	Beetroot	Joe Grundy
1st prize	Roses	Phil Archer
Unplaced	Chocolate cake	Pat Archer
1st prize	Wild flower photograph: Lady's bedstraw	Usha Gupta

Unplaced....................Wild Flower Photograph: ....Terry Booth
Wild Campion and foxgloves

⁓ 2003 ⁓
Overall winner: Bert Fry

1st prize ....Men Only Cakes: Lemon Drizzle ....Alistair Lloyd
(in fact one of Phil's entered by Alistair in error)

1st prize ....Gentleman's buttonhole ....Freda Fry

1st prize .... An unusual marmalade (ginger)...............Freda Fry
(had been rumoured to be nettle)

2nd prize......An unusual marmalade (lemon and quince) ...Jill Archer

Unplaced.................... An Unusual marmalade:...............Kirsty Miller
marmalade face pack

Unplaced......An Unusual marmalade: lemon and ginger ....Jill Archer

Unplaced.................... An Unusual marmalade: ....Jill Archer
lime and passion fruit

Unplaced..... An Unusual marmalade: brandy marmalade....Jill Archer

Unplaced......An Unusual marmalade: onion marmalade ....Jill Archer

Unplaced.......... An Unusual marmalade: apple brandy.. Clarrie Grundy

TALES FROM BONFIRE NIGHT

In the past, Bonfire Night has been held at Grey Gables, Brookfield and Home Farm. These days the festivities are held on the Village Green. Firewood is collected from around the village by volunteers, usually organised by Mike. In 1984, The Bull's front door was damaged by kids throwing bangers at it.

According to Joe, Bonfire Night is one of the best nights for poaching, because nobody takes any notice of bangs (shots). Peggy and others worry about their pets. Lynda checks the fire on the day for hibernating hedgehogs, though all she's ever found is a toad.

In 1991, Bonfire Night was the scene of a reconciliation for Sid and Kathy after her affair with Dave Barry. When Sid was burnt by a firework, Kathy bandaged his hand and called him 'my love'.

But a good time is not always had by all…

In 1993 the Carters had their own little bonfire at home. After her time in prison, Susan felt unable to join in with village events.

Ruth had her most miserable Bonfire Night in 2006: convinced David was sleeping with Sophie, she was torturing herself over agreeing to spend a night in Oxford with Brookfield herdsman Sam. Ignorant of this and innocent of any wrongdoing, David threw himself into preparations, helping to build the bonfire with Josh and Ben and generally being a great dad.

On Bonfire Night 2007, Ed had to coax a cowering Jack out of the gents at The Bull where he was hiding from what he thought was an air raid on Stirchley, his former home in Birmingham, where he'd been a fire watcher in the war.

TALES FROM
REMEMBRANCE SUNDAY

- There are trays of poppies for sale in: the Shop, The Bull, the Church, Grey Gables and Lower Loxley.
- Joe Grundy's cousin, Ted, signed up in Borchester at the age of 18. He was killed on the first day of the Somme.
- There is a 'Pullen' listed on the Ambridge war memorial – Mr Pullen's uncle who died at Passchendaele.
- One of Mr Pullen's first memories is his father's return from the Great War.
- Mr Pullen himself served in Burma in the Second World War.
- In 2006, Peggy spoke in church about her wartime experiences. She reflected that while everyone else got older, those who had died in the war never would.

- Marjorie Antrobus sold poppies for over thirty years and received a Long Service Medal from the British Legion for doing so.
- At Oliver's first Remembrance Day parade as a young subaltern, he had to wear a pair of size 12 shoes which were too big.
- Jack can remember his Stirchley pals – Norman Shillingford, who was killed in the Second World War, and Norman's brother Wilf, who came home with only one leg.
- Nigel has visited the Ypres battlefield where his Great-Uncle Rupert was killed.

HAPPY CHRISTMAS, DARLING: 1998

- Eddie gave Clarrie a boxed set of romantic novels.
- Clarrie's sister Rosie sent Joe a hand-knitted jumper but the sleeves were too long.
- Neil gave Susan a crystal fruit bowl.
- Alistair gave his new wife Shula (they were married on Christmas Eve) a heated device for scraping the ice off her car windscreen.
- Alistair gave Jill bubble bath.
- Alistair took Daniel to see Father Christmas.
- Kenton phoned from Australia.
- Bert's family came to visit him.
- Kate gave a Winter Solstice Party.
- Peggy and Jack gave George and Chris Christmas dinner at Grey Gables.

CHANCE REMARK

In April 1952, the Squire offered a sickbed-bound Mike Daly the use of his television set. His offer came to nothing as Blossom Hill Cottage, which Mike rented, didn't have electricity at the time, but it prompted Peggy's mother, Mrs P, into declaring that she'd like a television for the lonely winter evenings. Her friend and neighbour Walter Gabriel dismissed TV as 'all fiddle-faddling poppycock' but, in typical Walter style, ambitiously set about trying to make one for her. Baffled by the science, he finally had to admit defeat and Mrs P bought one. It was such a novelty in Ambridge that Mrs P invited Dan, Doris, Tom and Walter to a party to watch it. As they did, Mrs P commented that it would be nice to have someone like Gilbert Harding or Elizabeth Allan, then popular TV and radio personalities, to open the Ambridge church fete. Later that year, sure enough, Gilbert Harding did the honours and awed a star-struck Mrs P into a rare silence when he bought one of her lavender bags.

HYPNOTIC

At the Ambridge fete in 1965, the star turn, a hypnotist, managed to convince Brookfield farm worker Ned Larkin that the glass of water he'd given him to drink was actually gin. Under the influence of alcohol, or so he believed, Ned staggered about the stage and sang a rousing version of 'Show Me The Way To Go Home', but amazingly, the next day, had no hangover!

LYNDA SNELL'S
CHRISTMAS PRODUCTION 2008
∼⤬∼

JACK AND THE BEANSTALK

In 1998, Lynda's arch-rival Larry Lovell produced *Jack and the Beanstalk* as the village panto. Some counter-intuitive casting resulted in Tracy Horrobin as Jack and her mother Ivy as Jill, Eddie's mates Baggy and Snatch as Clarabelle the Cow, Freda Fry as the Fairy and Jack Woolley's handyman/chauffeur Higgs as Dame Trot. The Giant was played by Peter (the landlord of The Cat and Fiddle).

Ten years later, Lynda was determined to outdo the previous production, but her cast was dogged by ill-health and sheer dilettantism. After much swapping of parts, the eventual cast and crew list comprised:

Jack	Fallon Rogers (replacing Sabrina Thwaite)
Jill	Brenda Tucker (replacing Fallon)
Dame Trot	Mike Tucker (replacing Kenton)
Daisy The Cow	Clarrie (replacing Mike) and Eddie Grundy; then Lynda and Robert Snell
Tripe, the Butler	David Archer
Onions, the Cook	Kenton Archer
Voice of the Giant	Oliver Sterling
Giant's wife	Susan Carter
Market trader	Joe Grundy
Chorus including	Lily and Freddie Pargetter, Phoebe Tucker
Front of House	Kathy Perks, with help from Tom's pig-woman Hannah
Costumes	Jill Archer and Shula Hebden Lloyd
Music	Christopher Carter (replacing Fallon)
Prompt	Alice Aldridge (replacing Christopher)

| Stage Manager | Robert Snell with Alistair Lloyd and Daniel |
| Writer/Director | Lynda Snell |

A POTTED HISTORY OF THE FLOWER AND PRODUCE SHOW

～ 2004 ～

New Adult Class: 'Dress A Scarecrow'

(There was a new children's class for same in 2001)

1st prize	Ambridge Hall	Peruvian Llama herder
2nd prize	The Laurels	with Zimmer frame
4th prize	Woodbine Cottage (Barfords)	with rake
Other entries:	The Bull	drinking a pint of Shires
	Home Farm	eating strawberries

1st prize	Onions	Bert Fry
1st prize	Carrots	Bert Fry
1st prize	Beetroot	Bert Fry
1st prize	Gentleman's buttonhole	Jennifer Aldridge
1st prize	Men Only sponge cake	Robert Snell

CHILDREN'S SECTION

| 1st prize | Decorated welly | Josh Archer |

～ 2005 ～

Rivalry this year was between Phil and Jill and Bert and Freda –
the Archers triumphed.

1st prize	Courgette chutney	Lynda Snell
1st prize	Honey	Jill Archer
2nd prize	Runner beans	Jill Archer
3rd prize	Carrots	Jill Archer
Two 1st prizes	Unspecified	Phil Archer

Highly commended	Roses	Phil Archer
1st prize	Sponge cake	Clarrie Grundy

TEN EASTER TITBITS

1. The village shop carries a small stock of Easter Eggs.

2. As William's godmother, even-handed Caroline used to buy eggs for both William and Edward.

3. Vicar Janet Fisher was very fond of chocolate, something she shares with Shula.

4. Tom Forrest always supplied foliage and flowers for the church from his garden.

5. Even non-regular churchgoers are on the Easter flower rota (including Pat).

6. In 1996, the Bishop took the Easter Service in St Stephen's.

7. He also attended the service in 2001 as a gesture of support in the year of foot-and-mouth.

8. In 1997, Ambridge made a Peace Quilt for Easter.

9. Having been in prison for Christmas, Susan Carter was released at Easter.

10. In 1998, Daniel Hebden Lloyd was in hospital over Easter with what turned out to be juvenile rheumatoid arthritis.

HARVEST SUPPER: SWEET

- In 1995, the Harvest Supper coincided with Uncle Tom's 85th birthday. As guest of honour, he was presented with a framed family photo.
- October 2003, and 'Harvest Home' at Brookfield coincided with another birthday, this time Jill's. Betty made quiches, Pat and Tony gave ice cream, yoghurt, potatoes and leeks from which Jill made a leek, marrow and potato boulangère, eaten with Brookfield beef, while Phil presented her with a special birthday cake.
- Pat and Tony hosted the 2008 Harvest Supper as a thank you to the village for their support in seeing off Borchester Land's threat to turn their packhouse into a luxury home. It also coincided with the Grange Farm Open Day and prompted another thank you: from Oliver to Ed on his determination not to let the TB in the Grange Farm herd defeat him.

OUR SPEAKER TONIGHT

Over the years, the W.I. has enjoyed talks by:

- Mrs Antrobus on 'The Colourful Life of the Afghan'
- Usha Gupta on 'A Taste of India'
- Mrs Posnett on 'The Flower Garden in Winter'
- Phil Archer on 'Agriculture in Australia'
- Chaba Proganyi on 'Hungarian Rhapsody'
- Major Austen Bigsby on 'Patagonia and the Patagonians'
- Jennifer once filled in at short notice on 'The Problems and Secrets of a Writer's Life'

JOE GRUNDY'S GHOST WALK
STOP NUMBER FIVE: THE MILLENNIUM WOOD

There are two ghosts to remember here:

THE WORM OF AMBRIDGE

According to Joe, the Worm of Ambridge first appeared during the Civil War when a Roundhead drowned in a well and reappeared as a snake, crushing to death the poor farmer who couldn't understand why the water had become tainted and had foolishly lowered himself down to take a look. Bad things happen every time it appears, so village feelings ran high when, in the summer of 2007, a mysterious guest abandoned a snake at Grey Gables and it seemed to be making itself at home in Ambridge.

THE SCREAMING SKULL

Somewhat embellished by Eddie, what is fact is that, excavating for a picnic area in the summer of 2008, Eddie's digger uncovered a human skull. This was dated back to the Civil War, and Nigel speculated that it was that of the son of the Lower Loxley Hall steward, who'd been a pikeman fighting for the King. An excavation at the site turned up various other small items dating from the period such as part of a *morion* (helmet). Nigel, taking a proprietary interest, arranged for the human remains to be buried in a simple ceremony in the local churchyard.

TALES FROM FATHER'S DAY

- Depending on his relations with them at the time, Brian's daughters Alice and Kate usually phone him on Father's Day.
- Susan cooks Neil a roast dinner on Father's Day.
- In 1998, a tactless Kenton enclosed with Phil's card a

postcard sending warmer greetings to his friends at the pub than to his dad.

- ✹ After the revelation of Ruairi's existence, Alice threw the Father's Day card she'd bought Brian in the bin.
- ✹ In 2000, Josh gave David a toy farmer and farmer's wife and Pip gave him a china cow.
- ✹ In 1998, the year of his 70th birthday, Shula gave Phil some CDs and Daniel sang him the World Cup football song.
- ✹ In the same year, Elizabeth gave her dad the score of Tchaikovsky's 1812 and announced he'd be conducting the overture at the Summer Spectacular at Lower Loxley.
- ✹ In 1995, 2-year-old Pip made David a Father's Day card in the shape of a cricket bat and gave him a bag of chocolate buttons.

A POTTED HISTORY OF THE FLOWER AND PRODUCE SHOW

～ 2006 ～

'Green' Cake Class

1st prize	Pistachio Roulade	Jennifer
Highly Commended	Green Icing	Jill Archer
Unplaced	Hemp Flour Cake	Phil Archer

ENTRIES:

Florence fennel	Phil Archer

AMBRIDGE GOES GREEN

The 'green' cake class at the fete in 2006 caused much discussion – did it refer to the eventual colour, the wholesomeness of the ingredients, or both? Phil's and Jill's interpretations were wildly different, with Jill's green-iced confection at least getting a 'Highly Commended' – and her internet-sourced food colouring was, though lurid, all natural. Poor Ian, tasked with judging, tried to be polite about Phil's hemp flour effort, saying only that it was 'very dense' and had 'a curious aftertaste'. The real loser was Jazzer who, hearing that a hemp cake was to be auctioned off after the show, took it to be dope cake, bought it and scoffed the lot – to be left feeling pretty dense himself.

~ 2007 ~

1st prize ....Runner Beans ....Bert Fry
(Derek Fletcher tried to swap the labels during a mass evacuation
caused by a burst pipe in the village hall; despite his own rivalry
with Bert, Phil magnanimously swapped them back as
Bert's were definitely the best.)

ENTRIES:

Dahlias ....Derek Fletcher
Runner beans, ('Enorma') Florence fennel ....Phil Archer
Runner beans, ('Achievement') onions, marrows, potatoes ..... Bert Fry
Tomatoes .... Joe Grundy
Marrow ....Phoebe Tucker
Collage ....Phoebe Tucker

FETE ACCOMPLI

Minutes from Fete Committee meeting, 12 June 1975,
detailing responsibilities:

Jack Woolley	To judge Children's Fancy Dress
Harry Booker	In charge of publicity and competitive sideshows
Doris Archer/Nora Salt	Bottle Stall
George Barford	Liaison with Hollerton Town Band
	(and to play cornet solo)

Walter Gabriel	'Guess The Weight' stall
Haydn Evans	Coconut shy
Charles Harvey	To donate 1st prize for Talent Competition
	(£10 record token)

BOOTING BONANZA

The Grundys were typically quick to exploit the car boot craze, though with mixed results:

- Joe got off to a bad start in 1992 when he offered a field for a fundraising car boot sale for the church, but said he didn't know how much to charge. Usha pointed out he was supposed to be donating it.

- By 1996, Joe had learnt his lesson and loaned a field for 'The Great Grange Farm Car Boot' which was to raise money for the proposed village playground. Disaster struck, however, when Caroline's husband, Guy Pemberton, suffered a heart attack at the sale. He was only saved by the fortuitous presence of local doctor Richard Locke.

- It was perhaps tactless, then, of Eddie to put up posters shortly afterwards for 'The Biggest Boot Sale in Borsetshire' and inflame their new landlord, Guy's son Simon. But, in a rare moment of clemency, though in contravention of their lease, he granted permission for just the one. Its success inspired Joe and Eddie to persuade Shula, then agent for the Estate, that they might do 'just a couple' more.

- At the next sale, queuing cars were backed up all the way to the Dower House and callers to Radio Borsetshire, along with locals, voiced their displeasure. Shula gave Eddie written notice of a breach in their tenancy agreement and when Eddie blustered, Simon was quick to show his anger. He sent Shula to carry out a surprise inspection which uncovered twenty-eight items at fault; the disgruntled Grundys were promptly served with a Notice to Remedy and given three months to do the work.

TOWN TWINNING

The *entente* was *chaotique* as well as *cordiale* when Ambridge was ceremonially twinned with the French village of Meyruelle in September 1994. Omens were bad at the rehearsal when the tablecloths blew away and the bell peal came in late, despite being called in over Brian's two-way radio. The peal proved equally troublesome on the day, when ringer Ernie Bennett dropped his glasses at the crucial moment. Never ones for the simple life, Ambridge villagers had also organised a local history display (including a gin trap and a hay knife) and presented a 'Rural Reminiscences' play, with Lynda offering simultaneous translation for the bemused visitors. *Vive la difference...* or not?

GHOSTS OF AMBRIDGE:
SIR ANDREW RALFE

In 1976, Sid and Polly Perks bought Rose Cottage in Penny Hassett with a view to their eventual retirement. As it needed modernising, they decided it would be fun to take 'before' and 'after' photos but when they collected the first set, discovered that they'd somehow snapped a ghost.

Dan Archer recalled that, many years before, there had been a cottage nearby with the reputation of having been haunted by the ghost of Sir Andrew Ralfe, who had been killed in the Civil War in 1644. Investigations proved that the old cottage had been built of

Horton Stone… and one wall in Sid and Polly's cottage was also built from Horton Stone.

Annoyingly, as ever, there was a literalist to damp down the speculation. After examining the photo closely, Paul Johnson's fish-farm manager Percy Jordan claimed that the 'ghost' was no more than a puff of smoke. Polly was in heated denial but later remembered that there had in fact been a bonfire next door when Sid took the photo. It's still a good story, though.

THE AMBRIDGE CAROL

Dan and Doris were known for their musical evenings at Brookfield but, while their party pieces were 'Down The Vale' and 'When We Are Married', it was John Tregorran's tenor voice which used to accompany Doris in this seasonal song. Uncle Tom also used to sing a rousing solo version.

As I walked out one winter-time
To hear the robin sing,
From Lakey Hill the shepherds saw
The star that led to the King;
And Ambridge Vale was filled with song
The stars twinkled clear
And fields and frosty hedgerows rang
With angels' heavenly cheer.

CHORUS
The holly and the mistletoe,
The ivy green beside
The Yule-log and the gentle snow
This merry Christmas-tide.

The cattle lowed, the donkey brayed,
The Bull's welcome was warm
When Mary's child, in manager laid
Found shelter from the storm.
Because of Him, mankind is safe
From Death's powers cease:
And Bethlem's Crib to Ambridge brings
The gifts of Hope and Peace.

CHORUS
The holly and the mistletoe, etc.

The Kings adored, the shepherds kneeled
The animals bowed low,
Before my eyes was it revealed
Although so long ago.
And as I wandered round about
And over the hill,
The Ambridge bells were ringing out
The Christmas message still.

CHORUS
The holly and the mistletoe, etc.

So shovel chestnuts on the fire
And pass the punchbowl round,
'Tis warmer fare in farm or byre
Than on the frozen ground.
The gift of peace the season brings
To men of good cheer:
'A merry Christmas-tide my friends,
And a Happy New Year'.

CHORUS:
The holly and the mistletoe, etc.

AMBRIDGE GETS THE HUMPH

Fete day in 1957 was not only the very first time Phil spotted Jill (and filmed her on his cine camera), but was also notable because the fete that year was opened by jazz musician and wit Humphrey Lyttleton. To the screams of the newly discovered phenomenon of 'teen-agers' calling 'Good old Hump!', 'Get Hep!' and 'Blow That Horn, Man!' , these were his opening words:

'Good afternoon, Ladies and Gentlemen. You know as well as I do that opening church fetes is hardly my line of country but I'd like to say that I feel greatly honoured to have been asked to officiate at the ceremony this afternoon. Now the object of the exercise, as I understand it, is to raise money for the church roof... er... as usual! So I mustn't waste any time talking to you and keeping you from the very important job of spending all your cash at the many and varied stalls I can see all around. The vicar and his band of outlaws are simply aching to relieve you of all the money that's weighing down your pockets. Remember – we're taking from the rich to help the poor... church roof! This is the first time I've had the pleasure of visiting Ambridge – I hope it won't be the last. Maybe later on I can bring down the boys to a ball in the village hall... then that'll be needing a new roof, too! Now – every opera has its overture before it starts – no meet of the local hunt would be complete without the sound of the huntsman's horn. So let's declare Ambridge fete open – with full musical honours!'

Humph then played 'some flourishing bars on his trumpet' accompanied by 'teen-age shrieks and applause'.

A POTTED HISTORY OF THE FLOWER AND PRODUCE SHOW

⁓ 2008 ⁓

1st prize	Gentleman's buttonhole	Peggy Archer
1st prize	Honey	Jill Archer
3rd prize	Victoria Sponge	Jill Archer (overcooked)
1st prize	Harvest fruit cake	Sabrina Thwaite

(Actually one of Jill's acquired by Sabrina via the Swap Club.
Jill let her have her moment of glory in the hope that
Size-Zero Sabrina might actually eat a piece.)

Master Gardener .... Joe Grundy
(Vase of flowers and 3 kinds of vegetable)

Photography 'Village Life'
Highly commended...'Beehive Cluster' (stars in the sky)...Phil Archer
Disqualified (NAS)............'Village People' ....Lynda Snell
(Lynda's pictures were 'Not According to Schedule'
as they had been digitally manipulated)

Entries:

Carrots	Phil Archer
Runner beans	Phil Archer
Runner beans	Joe Grundy
Straightest runner bean	Bert Fry
Onions	Bert Fry
Marrow	Bert Fry

Gentleman's buttonhole .... Lilian Bellamy
Master Gardener .... Bert Fry

BUT IT'S WORTH IT

The Lent Appeal has raised money for:

- ❧   Colombian Street Children
- ❧   The Church Urban Fund
- ❧   Farmers in Rwanda
- ❧   The Blue Peter Appeal
- ❧   'Vicars on Wheels' in Malawi

WALTER'S WHEEZES

A staunch supporter of the Ambridge fete, throughout the 1960s Walter Gabriel came up with many money-spinning attractions – and christened them accordingly:

- ❧ Marmaduke, the ventriloquist's dummy – a perennial favourite

- ❧ Gabrielle, later Sarah (after an old girlfriend), a steam engine (1963)

- ❧ Pegasus, a hot-air balloon (1964)

- ❧ Rosie and her baby, Tiny Tim – elephants (1965)

- ❧ Mutt and Jeff – performing seals (1966)

SPILE-TROSHING

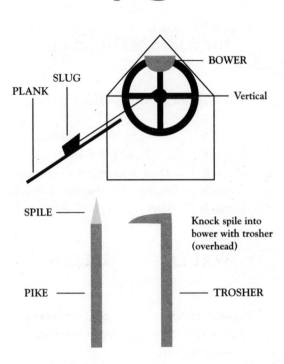

When a novel attraction was needed for the fete in 2000, Joe Grundy remembered the traditional game of spile-troshing. A 20 pound weight (slug) is attached with a rope to the axle of a cart wheel. The player has to use the trosher to flick the spile (the wooden cone from a beer barrel) into the bower (basket) as the wheel is turned. If the spile goes in on the first rotation, it's worth three points (a 'prime'). If the player misses, it's a 'blind' (no points).

Understand? Nor did most of the players. Helen's boyfriend, Greg, reckoned Joe had made the whole thing up and his instinct was proved right when Joe admitted as much. But by then several mystified players had already paid up for a go.

HAVE A CUPPA

At the 1982 Ambridge village fete, a cup of tea
in the tea tent cost 10 pence.

FARMERS' MARKETS

Borchester's Farmers' Market is on a Thursday twice a month;
Felpersham's weekly Friday Farmers' Market is one of the biggest in the
area. Darrington Farmers' Market is on a Monday and Hollerton's is on
Tuesdays and Fridays twice monthly.

GENERAL MARKET DAYS

Monday	Felpersham
Tuesday	Hollerton
Wednesday	Layton Cross
Friday	Borchester

ITEMS TO BE CONSUMED DURING THE 'BUSHTUCKER' TRIALS (2004 FETE)

Based around the *I'm A Celebrity…* idea, the test involved three levels
of increasing difficulty and disgustingness:

1. a plate of dry cream crackers and a tea bag
2. a plate of tripe
3. a plate of dog food, whilst holding a Chile
   Rose tarantula

Life
& Leisure

THE CRICKET CLUB

In the early days, the Cricket Club (President: the Squire, Vice-Presidents: George Fairbrother and Dan Archer) played its matches on the village green. Umpires in those times included Jeff Pope and Walter Gabriel and Phil Archer was on the Committee which planned the A.G.M. and Dinner, held at The Bull.

The site of the cricket pitch moved to Grey Gables in 1983. A plaque commemorates Jack Woolley's generous donation of the pavilion.

PUPPY REARING

In the 1950s, this was the advice given on rearing puppies:

Meals	Two a day
First meal	Bread and milk
Second meal	Biscuit meal moistened with gravy from bones, mixed with chopped offal, poor meat, etc.
Tonic	Mixture of castor oil and syrup of buckthorn
Scurf	To prevent scurfy coats mix black sulphur and home-made lard into an ointment

EAT YOUR WAY ROUND AMBRIDGE: KEEPER'S COTTAGE

Clarrie is a good plain cook, like her mother. Eddie loves her tripe and onions while Emma used to say Clarrie's Yorkshire pudding was better than Susan's. William was always a fan of Emma's sausage and mash and likes his roast potatoes cooked with rosemary. Joe's late wife Susan was a fearsome cook, too. She used to make her own clotted cream with a jug and a kettle, skin rabbits and make her own brawn and potted meats as well as an excellent pigeon pie. Her recipes, Joe recalls, used to involve a spoonful of Marmite in everything – though not, presumably, puddings.

ANIMALS OF AMBRIDGE

Biff	Brookfield's working sheepdog.
Scruff	(Alsatian cross) Daniel's dog, now living with Lynda.
Meg	William's gun dog. He started working her in September 1999.
Mitch	Greg's gun dog since 2001 – now looked after by William.
Fly	Home Farm's working sheepdog.

Bill and Ben	Jack and Peggy's cats, given to Peggy by Joe in November 2000 after the demise of her previous, much-loved cat, Sammy.
Eccles	The peacock who has lived at The Bull since 1993. Peacocks live on average for over 20 years and some as long as 40.
Maisie	Caroline's horse, given to Caroline by Guy for her 40th birthday in 1995.
Tolly	Debbie's Hanoverian Cross Thoroughbred horse. Tolly is short for Autolycus. Brian bought him for Debbie in 1992.
Bartleby	Joe's pony, acquired by Joe in 2002.
Spearmint	Alice's horse.
Benjamin	The donkey at the stables always commandeered for Palm Sunday.
Constanza and Wolfgang	Ambridge Hall's Llamas – a birthday present to Robert from Lynda.
Salieri	Their baby llama.
Barbarella	The Grundys' Berkshire pig, affectionately known as 'Miss Babs'.

Eddie has various ferrets which have included:
Mrs Archer (it was a 'jill' (female) ferret), Noah, Mrs Noah,
Leanne, Adelaide, Brooklyn and Romeo.

AMBRIDGE WEDDING BELLS
(AND BELLES)

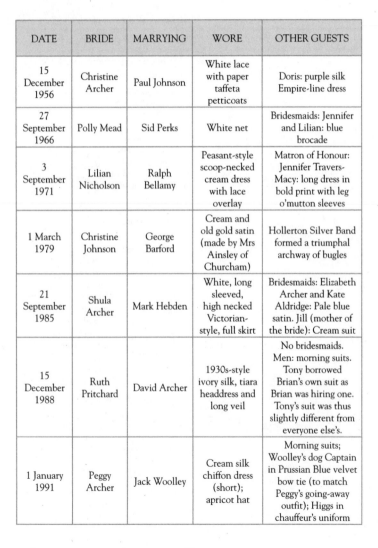

DATE	BRIDE	MARRYING	WORE	OTHER GUESTS
15 December 1956	Christine Archer	Paul Johnson	White lace with paper taffeta petticoats	Doris: purple silk Empire-line dress
27 September 1966	Polly Mead	Sid Perks	White net	Bridesmaids: Jennifer and Lilian: blue brocade
3 September 1971	Lilian Nicholson	Ralph Bellamy	Peasant-style scoop-necked cream dress with lace overlay	Matron of Honour: Jennifer Travers-Macy: long dress in bold print with leg o'mutton sleeves
1 March 1979	Christine Johnson	George Barford	Cream and old gold satin (made by Mrs Ainsley of Churcham)	Hollerton Silver Band formed a triumphal archway of bugles
21 September 1985	Shula Archer	Mark Hebden	White, long sleeved, high necked Victorian-style, full skirt	Bridesmaids: Elizabeth Archer and Kate Aldridge: Pale blue satin. Jill (mother of the bride): Cream suit
15 December 1988	Ruth Pritchard	David Archer	1930s-style ivory silk, tiara headdress and long veil	No bridesmaids. Men: morning suits. Tony borrowed Brian's own suit as Brian was hiring one. Tony's suit was thus slightly different from everyone else's.
1 January 1991	Peggy Archer	Jack Woolley	Cream silk chiffon dress (short); apricot hat	Morning suits; Woolley's dog Captain in Prussian Blue velvet bow tie (to match Peggy's going-away outfit); Higgs in chauffeur's uniform

29 September 1994	Elizabeth Archer	Nigel Pargetter	Cream antique lace	Bridesmaids: Debbie and Alice Aldridge, plus Rosie, daughter of one of Elizabeth's friends: pink bo-peep style. Jill (mother of the bride): Green jacket and green-grey print dress
7 May 2001	Hayley Jordan	Roy Tucker	White satin strapless, boned bodice, full skirt, with beading	Groom, best man (Tom Archer) and ushers: morning suit, with waistcoat and cravat in blue and gold
4 July 2002	Jolene Rogers	Sid Perks	Country and Western theme: White with turquoise trim, flounced and embroidered skirt, fringed waistcoat, appliqué shawl, white leather cowboy boots	Sid: white suit and bootlace tie: Jamie: fringed waistcoat and chaps on his trousers
27 August 2004	Emma Carter	William Grundy	White heavy satin, strapless, boned bodice, slim skirt. No veil.	Susan (mother of the bride): Brown polka-dot dress (like the one Julia Roberts wore in *Pretty Woman*) with cream jacket and accessories. Clarrie (mother of the groom): Peach three-quarter length jacket and skirt with a satin finish; hat with small veil (lucky charity shop find)
15 July 2009	Vicky Hudson	Mike Tucker	Strapless white full length dress, boned bodice, and net skirt.	Mike: new suit; Phoebe (who was ringbearer): a new dress; Brenda: the same suit she wore for Abbie's christening. All guests had corsages or buttonholes.

LYNDA'S CHILD SUBSTITUTES

Lynda has collected a variety of animals
since her move to Ambridge:

DOGS

- Hermes – a runtish Afghan puppy
- Scruff – used to be Daniel's dog but too boisterous around the horses at The Stables

GOATS

- Persephone
- Demeter

LLAMAS –
A BIRTHDAY PRESENT TO ROBERT (SUPPOSEDLY)

- Constanza
- Wolfgang
- And their baby Salieri

GLOVES OFF

Do real men wear gloves? Alistair's often to be heard snapping on a latex or rubber pair before performing a particularly intimate animal investigation, but it was when gambler Ryan returned an everyday pair which Alistair had left in Ryan's car that his new friend from Gamblers Anonymous, on seeing the set-up at The Stables, clocked just how well veterinary work pays. Typecasting aside, the fingerless gloves Joe habitually wears in the winter made him a shoo-in for Scrooge in Lynda's production of *A Christmas Carol.*

THE DOG WOMAN

- This was the name Joe and Eddie gave to Marjorie Antrobus.
- Her first appearance in Ambridge in 1984 was to give a talk to the Ambridge W.I.
- Its title was 'The Colourful World of the Afghan'. The audience were surprised to hear her eulogise about dogs. They had expected a travelogue.
- Marjorie's dogs were referred to as 'my gels'.
- The two most characterful were Bettina and Portia.
- A chance meeting between Portia and Jack Woolley's Staffordshire Bull Terrier, Captain, resulted in the birth of nine puppies.
- When David and Ruth were living with Marjorie, Portia gave birth to four puppies – on their bed.
- Bettina didn't like to get dirty. For 'walkies' on wet days, Marjorie would put freezer bags on the dog's feet to keep them mud-free and dry.
- Bettina died in 2002. A few days later Marjorie had the fall which led to her giving up her home.
- Both Portia and Bettina are buried in the garden at Nightingale Farm.

CHICKEN LICKEN

- Phoebe's three Silkies are called Snowdrop, Blossom and Alfred.
- Sid's daughter Lucy protested against the battery hen unit which Neil used to run in the village.

- An escaped hen from the battery unit was adopted by Lucy and Aunt Laura and christened Jessica or 'Superhen'.

- When someone in her office offered her £500 in sponsorship to do so, Usha did the Felpersham 10km run dressed as a chicken.

- Dan wasn't always a stick-in-the-mud. As early as 1953 he transferred his pullets from free range to deep litter.

- The Willow Farm hens lay Brown Speckled eggs.

- They were originally a shared enterprise between Neil and Betty Tucker, who wanted to put to good use her maturing 'nest egg' investment.

- The Lower Loxley Rare Breed hens are Derbyshire Redcaps.

- Pat used to keep a few hens at Bridge Farm.

- The hens at Brookfield are Jill's. They live in the orchard.

BULLS-EYE

Darts is still popular at The Bull, though the current team varies depending on availability. In 1989 the regular team was:

THE BULL
Neil (Captain)
David
Mike
Shula
Keith Horrobin
Tom Forrest

THE CAT AND FIDDLE
Eddie (Captain)
Snatch Foster
Baggy
Jolene
Fatty Partridge
Herbie

MARTHA WOODFORD'S RASPBERRY GIN

'If you have a good crop of raspberries, here's a nice way of using them up. To every 2lbs of fruit you need one pint of gin and 1lb of caster sugar.

'Hull the fruit and put it into a large jar. Add the gin and sugar and cover the top of the jar with kitchen foil. Stir often for a week to be sure that the sugar has dissolved. Leave for six months. Strain and bottle. Don't throw the raspberry pulp away – it makes a very heady trifle.'

GRUNDY PIGS

When Ed helped a hung over Neil with his pigs following Alan's stag night, he confided that he liked pigs: they'd always had them at Grange Farm. Not surprisingly, Joe was always on the scrounge for food for them. In 1977, claiming the area had used to be Common Land, he took four pigs foraging for acorns in the Country Park. But Jack Woolley – at that time perfectly astute – had also done his local history research. Quite so, he told Joe – but in return Joe owed him a day's labour. The disgruntled Grundy beat a hasty retreat.

EDDIE'S COUNTRY AND WESTERN OUTFITS

Eddie hasn't always slouched around in a grubby 'Shires' sweatshirt and a fleece. In his glory days as a C&W star in the late 1970s and early 1980s, he cut a dash in his stage clothes – two authentic cowboy shirts of different designs, a buckskin shirt, a frilled shirt with fringing and even one studded with rhinestones. Eddie's favourite, however, was his embroidered shirt. Those were the days...

EAT YOUR WAY ROUND AMBRIDGE: AMBRIDGE VIEW

Neil remembers Sunday teas at the Horrobins when he and Susan were courting, although, since Ivy Horrobin is a disastrous cook, the memories may be somewhat mixed. Susan used to say that her brothers and sister were the only kids at school who looked forward to school dinners. Susan herself is a good, if not always adventurous, cook. She panicked in the face of entertaining what she thought was going to be Christopher's Asian girlfriend, only to find that it was in fact posh Venetia ('Netia') Streatfield. Luckily her aubergine sambal was much appreciated. A loving if sometimes overprotective mum, Susan forbade Christopher from eating the jelly at the children's tea to celebrate the opening of the Dan Archer Memorial Playground in 1996 because of the possible BSE risk from the gelatine.

MEASURING OF PIGS

Dan's farmhand, Simon Cooper, had an infallible guide for assessing whether a pig was up to bacon weight: forget weighing, simply measure round the girth. (A pig's girth is just behind its forelegs.) Allow 100lbs for the first 3 feet of girth and 10lbs for every extra inch. The 1950s ideal for fat bacon would certainly, however, differ from today's – so perhaps Tom and Jazzer had better not try it.

THE AMBRIDGE WANDERERS FOOTBALL TEAM

The football pitch in Ambridge was behind Mrs P's cottage. The team colours were green and white stripes. The team of 1975 were:

Harry Booker (Captain)
Mike Tucker (Goalkeeper)
Tony Archer (Forward)
Richard Adamson
Colin Drury
Bobby Waters
Gordon Armstrong
Sid Perks
Peter Stevens
Neil Carter
Gerry Goodway

FOOT(BALL) NOTE:
THE AMBRIDGE LADIES FOOTBALL TEAM (1975)

Pat Archer (Captain)
Jennifer
Betty Tucker
Polly Perks
Mary Pound
Susan Harvey
Christine Johnson
plus unspecified others

Matches Played:
Ambridge Ladies v Borchester Ladies (lost 3 – 2)
Referee: Brian Aldridge
Ambridge Ladies v Ambridge Wanderers (a draw!)

AMBRIDGE WANDERERS F.C.
FIXTURE LIST – SEASON 1975-6

1975

Sept.	6	Hollerton	A	Draw	1 – 1
	13	Churcham	H	Lost	0 – 2
	20	Netherbourne	H	Lost	0 – 1
	27	Claydon	A	Won	3 – 2
Oct.	4	Layton Cross	H	Won	3 – 0
	11	Heybury	A	Draw	2 – 2
	18	Perivale	A	Lost	1 – 4
	25	Borbury	H	Won	3 – 1
Nov.	1	Plympton, Sussex	A	Won	1 – 0
		(First Round of Comp.)			
	9	Little Croxley	H	Draw	2 – 2
	16	Penny Hassett	A	Draw	0 – 0
	25	Darrington	A	Lost	3 – 4
Dec.	6	Felpersham	H	Won	2 – 1
	13	Marbrick, Lancs.	H	Won	4 – 3
		(Second Round of Comp.)			
	20	Edgeley	A	Lost	0 – 2

1976

Jan.	3	Hollerton	H	Won	2 – 1
	10	Churcham	A	Draw	1 – 1
	17	Jephcott, Yorks.	A	Draw	2 – 2
		(Third Round of Comp.)			

(Ambridge win the replay at Home 1 – 0. They had to
borrow the Borchester pitch which has floodlights.
Replay on Wednesday 21st Jan.)

	23	Claydon	H	Draw	2 – 2
	30	Netherbourne	A	Won	4 – 2
Feb.	7	Layton Cross	A	Lost	2 – 3
	14	Swambridge, Kent	A	Won	2 – 1
		(Fourth Round of the Comp.)			
	21	Heybury	H	Lost	0 – 1
	28	Perivale	H	Won	1 – 0
March	6	Felpersham	A	Draw	0 – 0
	13	Borchester	H	Lost	1 – 2
		(Fifth Round of Comp.)			

(Borchester knocked out in quarter finals. So impressed
with some of the Ambridge players, they tried to poach.)

	20	Penny Hassett	H	Draw	0 – 0
	27	Darrington	H	Win	5 – 2
April	3	Borbury	A	Win	4 – 0
	10	Edgeley	A	Draw	2 – 2
	17	Norgate	H	Lost	0 – 3

<u>AMBRIDGE WANDERERS</u>
<u>FIXTURE LIST – 1976-7</u>

At the A.G.M. of the Ambridge F.C., it was decided not to enter
the Crocker Memorial Shield Competition this season, on
financial grounds. Harry Booker was re-elected team captain
and coach, and Tony Archer was appointed as vice-captain.

<u>1976</u>

Sept.	11	Darrington	A	Won	1 – 0
	18	Loxley Barrett	H	Draw	2 – 2
	25	Felpersham	A	Lost	0 – 3
Oct.	2	Churcham	H	Won	2 – 0
	9	Rimford	H	Won	3 – 2
	16	Clayhampton	A	Draw	1 – 1
	23	Hungerton	A	Lost	0 – 4
	30	Ansley	A	Won	1 – 0
Nov	7	Banthorpe	H	Won	3 – 2
	14	Lyttleton	H	Draw	3 – 3
	21	Edgecombe	A	Lost	2 – 3
	28	Glenbrook	A	Lost	0 – 2
Dec.	5	Ilton	H	Won	5 – 0
	12	Madely	H	Draw	2 – 2
	19	Neesfield	A	Won	1 – 0
	26	Special Boxing Day Fixture against a Scratch			

Team from Borchester. Abandoned after an hour's play because
of the condition of both teams.

<u>1977</u>

Jan.	1	Darrington	H	Draw	2 – 2
	8	Loxley Barrett	A	Lost	0 – 3
	15	Felpersham	H	Lost	1 – 4
	22	Churcham	A	Lost	2 – 3
	29	Rimford	A	Won	4 – 3
Feb.	5	Clayhampton	H	Won	6 – 1
	12	Hungerton	H	Lost	1 – 2
	19	Ansley	H	Lost	0 – 4
	26	Banthorpe	A	Won	1 – 0
March	5	Lyttleton	A	Draw	2 – 2
	12	Edgecombe	H	Draw	0 – 0
	19	Glenbrook	H	Lost	0 – 1
	26	Ilton	A	Won	3 – 2
April	2	Madely	A	Lost	0 – 4
	9	Neesfield	H	Won	5 – 2
	16	to be arranged			

EAT YOUR WAY ROUND AMBRIDGE: GLEBE COTTAGE

The Glebe Cottage kitchen has seen some keen cooks over the years. Doris was famed for her baking and preserves: Dan was especially fond of her beef and mushroom pie. Before her marriage, Jill was a demonstrator of cookery and appliances and is a renowned cake-maker, her chocolate and carrot cakes being particular favourites with the family. Phil's not afraid to experiment and has a state-of-the-art mixing machine, but he had a disastrous attempt at making marmalade in 2009 when his jam thermometer snapped off in the pan.

THE LAW IS AN ASS?

In 1980, the hunt was disrupted by saboteurs, including a Mr and Mrs Jarrett from Waterley Cross. Engaging Mark Hebden as their solicitor, the couple claimed they'd been assaulted by hunt members, resulting in bruised ribs and swollen hands. Mark defended the Jarretts in the Magistrates Court on a charge of criminal damage (for spray-painting a fence), bringing him into conflict with both Shula (his girlfriend) and her father, Phil, Chairman of the bench. When the *Borchester Echo* quoted a furious Mark as saying that magistrates were no more than 'socially accepted amateurs', he was banned from Brookfield. Phil had to give in, however, when Mark appealed on behalf of the Jarretts and won. Mark's proposal to Shula could also have had something to do with it.

EAT YOUR WAY ROUND AMBRIDGE: THE VICARAGE

Alan is a good cook and has passed on the enthusiasm to his daughter Amy, a vegetarian. Usha, on the other hand, is no great cook – when she lived on her own, her Aunty Satya used to send food to her through the post. She is, however, very fond of Pat's ice cream and enjoyed the mountains of carbohydrates she had to eat while training for the marathon. Alan has a weak spot for mince pies, and for his ex-mother-in-law Mabel's cooking. She makes a very warming ginger cake and, when visiting, often cooks Jamaican rice and peas for Sunday dinner.

SEVEN TITBITS FOR DEDICATED FOLLOWERS OF FASHION

- Nigel's party trick used to be undoing girls' bras through their clothes.
- The most comfortable thing Lower Loxley gardener Titcombe owns are, he says, his working boots.
- John Archer always wore gumboots for work. He knew Hayley was serious about him when she bought herself a pair.
- Lynda never wears jeans.
- At the height of her affair with Sid, one of Jolene's favourite outfits was a zebra print skirt and matching fun fur hat.
- When Usha despaired of finding a wedding dress before the autumn stock came in, Ruth promised her she would not let her get married in tweed.
- In 1984, Elizabeth was a size 10.
- Dan always wore a nightshirt, never pyjamas.
- When Bert started his guiding work at Lower Loxley, Alan helped him choose a pair of chinos, a shirt and a gilet. Bert was particularly impressed with all its pockets.

MR FAIRBROTHER'S SHOOT

In 1956, George Fairbrother reckoned his shoot cost him £400–£500 a year to run, this cost including Tom Forrest's wages, the cost of rearing and beaters. To make more of a profit, the following year he brought in four more paying guns at £50 per head.

A BIGGER SPLASH

Despite being landlocked, Ambridge folk do occasionally take to the water. In the early 1980s, in yet another disastrous attempt at finding a career, Nigel was briefly a swimming-pool salesman. He sold Jack Woolley the outdoor swimming pool at Grey Gables, though the deal hit a hiatus when Jack fell off a roof before signing the contract.

Nigel also sold Derek Fletcher his fishpond, now guarded by a phalanx of gnomes.

- Before the Health Club opened at Grey Gables the young men and women of Ambridge used to swim in Arkwright Lake, then owned by the Squire.
- When Phil was about 10, a boy called Johnny Bray drowned there.
- Apart from the Health Club, the nearest swimming baths are in Borchester.
- Jennifer and Brian were so frustrated at delays in the construction of the Home Farm swimming pool that they took themselves off on holiday to the Seychelles.
- When Ruairi came to Home Farm he couldn't swim, something else for Jennifer to worry about.
- The first time Shula saw Richard Locke without his clothes on was at the Grey Gables pool. Though he was Usha's boyfriend, Shula and Richard started an affair.

ONE MAN AND HIS DOG

Apart from Peggy, the great love of Jack Woolley's life was his Staffordshire Bull Terrier, Captain. Acquired by a lonely Jack in 1978 as a 3-month-old puppy, his unruly behaviour, in puppyhood and beyond, was a constant source of irritation to gamekeepers Tom Forrest and George Barford. Captain further disgraced himself in 1984 by eating Susan and Neil Carter's wedding cake, which was waiting to be iced by Grey Gables chef Jean-Paul. Over the years, a rich diet of braised calves' liver, smoky bacon crisps and biscuits from his doting master's afternoon tea tray considerably slowed Captain down and his favourite occupation became snoozing in front of the fire. He always enjoyed a full Christmas dinner although Peggy (once on the scene) drew the line at the plum pudding and brandy butter.

In 1988, Captain somehow summoned up the energy and agility for an amorous encounter with one of Marjorie Antrobus's Afghan hounds and nine interesting puppies – definitely not to Kennel Club standards – were born.

Captain died (of a broken heart?) while Peggy and Jack were on their honeymoon in 1991. He was laid to rest next to the golf course. His headstone is inscribed: 'Well done, thou good and faithful servant.'

EAT YOUR WAY ROUND AMBRIDGE: HOME FARM

Before she went to University, all Alice could cook were sponge cake, chocolate chip cookies and pasta bake. When Peggy gave her a student cookbook, she and Christopher made (and pigged out on) chocolate brownies. Jennifer is an excellent cook, much appreciated by Brian. She also makes delicious homemade lemonade, much appreciated by all the farm workers at harvest. When Debbie's home, her favourite pudding, apple crumble, is sure to be on the menu.

BETTY TUCKER'S ADVICE ON GOATS

If a goat has eaten a poisonous substance, such as rhododendron leaves, dose it with a mixture of bicarbonate of soda and melted lard to settle the stomach.

JACKET REQUIRED

- In 1976, one of Joe's favourite outfits was an ex-County Council donkey jacket.
- In 1988, David bought Elizabeth a grey satin jacket to make up for smashing her owl ornament when moving his and Ruth's double bed into Elizabeth's bedroom.
- Brian has a smart green jacket which he was wearing one birthday when he was scathing to Jennifer about her interest in homeopathy.
- Jennifer got her own back by pretending her 'vintage' knitted jacket had been made by Granny P. In fact she'd bought it – at considerable expense.
- When Joe tried 'Lonely Hearts' dating in 1987, Marjorie gave him an old Harris tweed jacket that had belonged to her late husband Teddy.
- When Phil wore a shabby jacket to Smithfield in 1989, Jill was very embarrassed.
- In 1991, Debbie persuaded Jennifer into buying a brightly coloured jacket which they both could 'share' – though it was clear who was going to get most use out of it. Debbie wore it to Joe Grundy's surprise 70th birthday party.
- In 1994, Elizabeth was furious to find a charity sticker had left a mark on her suede jacket.
- Marjorie knitted matinee jackets for Phoebe.

- When romancing Mildred Summerskill in 2008, Joe splashed out on a new jacket from a charity sale at a tea dance. He wore it to Marjorie Antrobus's funeral.
- Tom became a suspect in a GM crop trashing in Northamptonshire when his then girlfriend Kirsty was arrested there wearing his denim jacket. Tom's bank statement was in the pocket.
- Jenkins in Felpersham do a good line in gentlemen's jackets.
- For Christmas in 2004, Sid and Jolene gave Jamie a helmet and a reflective jacket to go with his bike.

MARJORIE ANTROBUS'S ZHUG (YEMENITE PICKLE)

1 tsp black peppercorns
1 tsp caraway seeds
3 – 4 fat cardamom pods
4 strong dried hot (chilli) peppers soaked in water for 1 hour
1 whole head garlic
Bunch of fresh coriander
Olive oil
Salt to taste

TRADITIONAL METHOD:

Pound the peppercorns, caraway seeds and cardamom seeds in a pestle and mortar. Add the drained chopped chillies (remove seeds unless you can tolerate real heat), peeled and chopped garlic, and pound again. Stir through the finely chopped coriander, loosen with olive oil and add salt to taste.

QUICK METHOD:

Place spices, garlic, chillies (prepared as above) and coriander in a food processor. Add the olive oil while motor is running. Finally add salt to taste.

(Marjorie's recipe uses a *huge* amount of garlic.
When eating, make sure you're among friends!)

HOLLOWTREE BOARS

In the 1980s, the Brookfield pig unit at
Hollowtree was home to several boars, each with a personality
all his own and a suitably evocative name:

- Playboy I
- Playboy II
- Playboy III
- Cromwell
- Monty
- Hercules

A THOUGHFUL GIFT

- For his birthday in 2002, Debbie and husband Simon
  gave Brian a hand-painted silk tie.

- Arriving home on leave from the Merchant Navy in
  1975, Kenton presented Shula with a grass skirt from
  Tahiti for a birthday present. (He'd in fact bought it in
  Sydney.) She was busy knitting him a scarf at the time.

- On Dan's birthday in 1983, he received a maroon
  cardigan from Shula, a book on roses and a radio from
  Phil and Jill and a tobacco pouch from David. Dan's
  cardigan was size 42.

TALES FROM THE
AMBRIDGE DARTS TEAMS

- Kathy once stood in for Shula, and The Bull won the match.
- Since his accident, Mike plays better with one eye than he ever did with two.
- The Viking trophy was presented by Lilian. It's a Viking warrior made of brass.
- It is competed for every year in the 'Bellamy Friendly'.
- Until its demise as a pub, The Cat and Fiddle won the trophy more often than The Bull.
- Having won it in 1982, the Cat mislaid the trophy. It was later found in their yard.
- The Cat also won the Viking in 1980.
- The Bull darts night used to be a Thursday.
- The dart board has doors that open to the side: the score is written on them.
- When Jamie Perks was a baby, Sid kept a record of his feed times and weight on the dartboard doors.

A CULINARY BREAKTHROUGH

At their wedding reception in 1957,
Phil and Jill had a running buffet instead of a sit-down meal.
The idea was revolutionary at the time.

IT STARTED WITH A... COAT

Julia Pargetter's first present from her future husband Gerald was a fox fur coat. In the early 1940s, he saw her on stage in chilly Bridlington, and appeared at the stage door with a red rose. The next day a box appeared. It contained the coat and a note: 'To warm your beautiful heart as you have warmed mine.' Julia kept the coat until her death, though she donated a less favoured one (an anniversary present – by then maybe the magic had gone?) to an Ambridge jumble sale. Fortunately she was not in Ambridge in 1986 when Pat was often to be seen in a T-shirt with the slogan: 'Fur coats are worn by beautiful animals and ugly people.'

HORSES

- Christine's horse Midnight was the cause of Grace Archer's death in the stables fire: Grace ran back in to save the horse.
- Dan bought Midnight on the advice of Reggie Trentham
- Matt Crawford has owned race horses.
- When Paul Johnson's horse Christina was running at Scowell Bradon, he asked Christine along for luck
- Paul himself rode Monarch at the Heybury Point-to-Point in 1958.
- Jack Woolley once owned a race horse called Grey Silk
- Ralph Bellamy and Lilian grew closer when he commissioned a portrait of her on his horse, Red Knight, which she'd ridden to victory in the Ladies' Race at the South Borsetshire Point-to-Point.
- Show-jumper Ann Moore, seeing Shula riding her horse Mr Jones, was so impressed she thought Shula might make a competition rider.

❧ In 1987, Brian had a 75 per cent share (Christine held the other quarter) in a hunter called Hassett Hill Two Timer or 'Tootsie'. Ironically, it had originally been owned by Brian's one-time flame Mandy Beesborough and was frequently ridden by another, Caroline Bone (now Sterling).

EAT YOUR WAY ROUND AMBRIDGE: BROOKFIELD

Whilst frozen pizza and jacket potatoes are still staples on the menu, Ruth's cooking has steadily improved over the years, though she still finds it stressful cooking for Jennifer, or any other good cook. Her ingenuity was tested by Pip's 'Within Five Miles' Lenten diet in 2009 but luckily cauliflower cheese, which the Brookfield kids love, was still a possibility under the regime. David meanwhile cooks a 'special casserole', a famous curry and can also cook Spaghetti Bolognese – he made this for the children the night Ruth was due to have her tryst in Oxford with their herdsman Sam.

A NOT-SO-MAD HATTER

Over the years, childless Martha Woodford knitted hats for all the village children. Roy Tucker's was yellow.

AMBRIDGE CRICKET TEAM

1976
Harry Booker
Brian Aldridge
Phil Archer
Tony Archer
Neil Carter
Sid Perks
Gordon Armstrong
Peter Stevens
Richard Adamson
Bobby Waters
Gerry Goodway

Reserves:
Steve Manson
Charles Harvey
Umpire: Tom Forrest

1987
Sid
David
Tony
Brian
Nelson
Neil
Mike
Eddie
Nigel Pargetter (having a brief flirtation with cricket)
Mark Hebden (now married to Shula. Had previously captained
Penny Hassett, so a coup for Ambridge)
Robert Snell (incomer but welcomed as M.C.C. member)

1999

Sid (Player/Manager)

Alistair (Captain)

David

Robert

Duncan (friend of Robert's)

Neil

Tom

Tony

Eddie

Roy

William

AMBRIDGE CRICKET TEAM 2009

Sid	Manager
Phil, Bert, Robert	Cricket Committee
Bert, Sid and Phil	Umpires (trained)
Neil	Groundsman
Alistair	Team Captain and Wicket Keeper
David	Good all rounder. Spin bowler and good batsman
Adam	Very good batsman and a good catch
Roy	Good batsman – if you want someone to hit a 6, Roy's your man
Neil	Put in against advice and took four wickets in five overs
Tom	A reasonable all-rounder but doesn't always attend nets
Christopher	Good player but has a tendency to hammer the ball
Duncan	Good, doesn't mind about batting orders
Stuart Graeme	Sports teacher at Loxley Barrett; athletic, good fielder

Robert	Getting on a bit but solid standby
Barry Simmonds	No notable traits
William	Good batsman, recently rejoined the team
Richard Thwaite	Keen supporter and occasional player
Eddie	Reserve if really desperate
Tony	Reserve if really, really desperate!

MUCH-LOVED AMBRIDGE CANINES (1964)

TOM FORREST
His much-loved dog JUDY, a spaniel,
having died in January 1961, she was replaced by a Labrador.

PHIL ARCHER
TIMUS, a corgi, a present from Walter Gabriel
and Bill Sawyer after Grace's death in 1955.

WALTER GABRIEL
BUTCH, a bulldog, a present from Debbie Glover in 1958.
He had to be put down in 1972.

JACK AND PEGGY
TURPIN, a boxer

MRS TURVEY
FELICITY, a terrier

DORIS ARCHER
TRIGGER, a Jack Russell. Born 28 December 1964,
he had to be put down in October 1976.

HAZEL TRENTHAM (LATER HAZEL WOOLLEY)
HONEY, a Bassett Hound. Given to her on her 10th birthday
(15 February 1966) but shot in January 1968 for sheep worrying.
Replaced 15 February 1968 by TROUNCER
(again nicknamed HONEY).

MRS SCROBY'S CURE FOR RHEUMATICS

According to Mrs Scroby:

Add a teaspoonful of mustard to a pint of beer,
boil it up and drink it as hot as you can bear.

(But treat with caution: Dr Cavendish, Ambridge's doctor in the
1950s, was driven to tell the well-intentioned but meddlesome
woman that her so-called cure for adder-bites was worse than useless).

COUNTRY PURSUITS

The combined effects of the 'really good skunk' Jazzer had
provided and the fact that it was close to April Fool's Day reduced
Ed, Fallon and Jazzer to helpless giggles when they encountered
Ed's brother William drey-poking in April 2004. Destroying
squirrels' nests with long poles is a legitimate activity on the part
of gamekeepers to rid themselves of the predatory creatures but,
though Fallon had a pang for the displaced squirrels, to Ed it
simply proved once again that William was a loser who didn't
deserve Emma, with whom Ed was secretly in love but whom
Will was to marry later that year.

EAT YOUR WAY ROUND AMBRIDGE: THE BULL

The Bull's cook, Freda Fry, is a legend in her own lunchtime. In the ultimate accolade, even Grey Gables chef Ian thinks that Freda's cooking is good, while Kenton claims that life always looks better after one of her steak and kidney pies. Her Yorkshire puddings are excellent and she has her own secret recipe for apple turnover. Not generally one for experiments (she's been using the same jam jars for 25 years), Freda's trip to India did, however, inspire her to make chutney. If Freda's not on duty, however, all is not lost: Sid makes a very good scrambled egg.

FOUR RANDOM FACTS ABOUT SOUP

1. One of the constituents of Kenton's fake blood which ruined a Chinese silk carpet at Lower Loxley one Halloween was Mrs Pugsley's borscht.

2. 'Lisa's lettuce soup' was a staple on the wine bar menu during the 1980s.

3. Pat was stirring a pan of soup when she finally broke down in the aftermath John's death.

4. Ruth offers a choice of soups when taking flasks out to the field to David and casual workers – tomato or mushroom are the safe staples.

EAT YOUR WAY ROUND AMBRIDGE: THE STABLES

Jim Lloyd doesn't cook; there hasn't been much point, he says, since Alistair's mother died. Shula, on the other hand, is a good cook who excels at puddings, while Alistair is a dab hand with Crepes Suzette and likes a slug of vodka in his consommé. Daniel likes Kenton's extra special omelette.

A TRUE SHEPHERD

Bert always claims that you can tell a true shepherd by the look in his eye: a light-coloured ring round the pupil, just like a sheep. Bert reckons David has it.

LIKE FATHER, LIKE SON

Cardigans have always spelt trouble in the Archer family. In the 1970s, Dan sought advice from Clarrie and her mum Lizzie Larkin to help choose a surprise present for Doris – a cashmere cardigan. Unfortunately, the colour was the last one Doris would have chosen. Happily she managed to change it at Underwoods for a green one, only to discover that the original had been bought in Benson's sale. Phil had no more luck with luxury fabrics, managing to shrink and pink Jill's cream cashmere cardigan in the wash while she was on holiday in Sidmouth. He thought he'd got away with replacing it, but had to confess in the end as the buttons were slightly different.

ON THE HUNT

Ambridge folk continue to hunt within the law. Notable past outings include:

- On Helen's first outing she led the hunt across Tony's carrot field.

- In 1991, the hunt went through Willow Farm, flattening fences and letting the pigs out. Betty thought her trashed kitchen was Mike's handiwork (he was severely depressed at the time). It was almost a relief to find that the pigs were to blame.

- In January 1994 the hounds went through the Grey Gables pheasant covers.

- In 2000, Oliver's first contact with Brookfield was to introduce himself as Joint Master and seek permission for the hunt to cross their land.

- Graham Ryder had a scare when he rode Marcellus, a large and unruly horse. After half a mile of acrobatics, Ryder was unseated.

- There was no hunting in 2001 owing to foot-and-mouth disease.

- Keith Speller is the other Joint Master.

- Matt's attempts to raise his profile with the local squirearchy in 2004 by means of riding lessons and attendance at the Hunt's Puppy Show did not succeed. Lilian was not impressed when one of the pups used her as a lamp post.

EAT YOUR WAY ROUND AMBRIDGE: WILLOW FARM

After Betty's death, Mike realised he had to learn to cook, and Brenda gave him some lessons. (She fondly remembers her mum showing her how to make chocolate brownies.) Mike's new wife Vicky loves spoiling him with a nice meal and Hayley is a good cook, too.

BORSETSHIRE'S NEXT TOP MODEL?

Peggy organised a fashion show at Grey Gables in 1998 aimed at the more 'mature' end of the market. Clothes were provided by Underwoods and the money raised went towards repairs to St Stephen's church bells.

Peggy modelled a flouncy, sequinned dress which she hated; to her horror, Jack liked it so much that he bought it for her. Joe modelled an elegant suit while Bert was resplendent in pyjamas and dressing gown – to the chagrin of Noel Coward fan Larry Lovell.

The music was another bone of contention, with Lynda bizarrely suggesting Chumbawumba and Julia (less bizarrely) Gershwin. Larry Lovell (predictably) wanted Noel Coward and Jack (equally predictably) the Tommy Croker Band. Finally, Marjorie's suggestion of Glenn Miller won the day.

The event was still more successful than the fashion show held by Elizabeth and Sophie when they were briefly in the fashion business together in the mid 1980s:

- Betty Tucker, who was down on her luck as Mike had gone bankrupt, was offered a paltry amount to sew for them.

- Neither of their fathers would back them with the £10,000 needed to set up a shop.

- Nelson came up with the money to stage fashion shows as a prelude to opening a shop.

- The first fashion event took place at Brookfield.

- Sophie had to take over from Jennifer as compère when Jennifer got drunk. She had just found out about Brian and Caroline's affair a few years previously.

- Caroline, mortified, left early.

- Susan Carter and Shula were models.

- Clarrie ordered a black dress which Eddie ended up having to pay for.

SOME CRICKET TEAMS IN THE SOUTH BORSETSHIRE LEAGUE

Borchester Green Old Boys
Borchester Old Boys
Borchester Mills
Darrington
Edgeley
Hollerton
Layton Cross

Little Croxley
Loxley Barrett
Netherbourne
Penny Hassett
Wimberton
Waterley Cross
Westbury

EAT YOUR WAY ROUND AMBRIDGE: BRIDGE FARM

Tony can't cook, so it's as well that Pat can, though not according to Brian, who claims her food gives him wind. He doubtless, therefore, avoided her homemade soup which was very popular after the Shepherds' Pageant at Christmas in 1992. Helen's ex, Greg, could cook – he could even make pastry.

CHARITY BEGINS...

Both Clarrie and Susan are fans of charity shop finds. Susan, who loves Neil in a tie, has amassed quite a collection for him at reasonable prices, while Clarrie scours the Save the Children shop in Borchester for bargains. She was delighted to find Eddie a suit there for his visit to Auntie Hilda in Aberdeen in 1992. The £15 price tag was a good investment: Aunt Hilda later left Will several thousand pounds. A charity shop wasn't good enough, however, for a suit for Clive Horrobin's court appearance. Neil was horrified when he found out that Susan intended ordering her wayward brother a suit from a catalogue for the occasion – at her own expense.

NOT UNDER MY ROOF

Nigel's father temporarily threw him out when he found Nigel had used a bottle of his best vintage port to make Cumberland sauce for duck. Nigel was forced to seek refuge at Tim Beecham's grotty flat until Shula begged for him to be allowed to stay at Brookfield.

EAT YOUR WAY ROUND AMBRIDGE: THE LODGE

Jack likes his scones with currants, whereas Peggy prefers hers plain, though she generally has a sweet tooth and was famous for her blackberry jam. She also cooks a superb Beef Wellington.

SINGLE WICKET CRICKET COMPETITION

The annual competition is in memory of keen cricketer Mark Hebden, Shula's first husband, who died in 1994. The competition is often, but not always, played on the late May Bank Holiday Monday. It's open to anyone, including outsiders, which explains appearances in 2002 by Kate's husband, Lucas Madikane, and in 2006 by Alice Aldridge's then boyfriend, Hungarian fruit picker Lajos. He'd never played cricket before – and it showed – but everyone expected

South African Lucas to be a cricketing force to be reckoned with. He was out for a duck.

For the uninitiated, 'single wicket' refers not to the stumps (a common misconception) but to the fact that it's a knockout competition involving individuals rather than teams. The actual rules are the same as for any game of cricket. After the first-round knockout, eight players remain and play against each other until two are left to contest the final. Sometimes the semi-finals and final will comprise three and four overs respectively. Fielding is done by the other players on a rotational basis.

The winner receives the Mark Hebden Memorial Trophy, which is always presented by Shula. The inscription reads: 'The Mark Hebden Memorial Trophy. In Memory of a Talented Player and a Valued Friend.' Sid has a duplicate, kept at The Bull, with a slightly different inscription: 'The Mark Hebden Memorial Trophy. In Memory of a Talented Player and a Trusted Friend.' The first winner, John Archer, mislaid the trophy and, thinking he'd got the wording right, had a replacement made, only for the original to turn up.

As 2009's triumph for Brenda Tucker reveals, it's not necessarily the best cricketers whose names get engraved on the trophy, though the multiple showings of past and current cricket team members indicate that playing regularly for the team is hardly a hindrance. Women, in fact, have often provided some upsets. Clarrie got off to a storming start in the very first competition in 1994, as did vicar Janet Fisher in 1998. Neil was embarrassed to be bowled out by Hayley Tucker in 1997 and, long before she bowled over Brian, Siobhan Hathaway was the undoing, in two successive years, 1999 and 2000, of Tony and then Tom.

NAMES AND DATES ENGRAVED ON THE MARK HEBDEN TROPHY

30TH MAY 1994
Winner: John Archer

29TH MAY 1995
Winner: John Archer

27TH MAY 1996
Winner: Roy Tucker

26TH MAY 1997
Winner: Richard Locke

25TH MAY 1998
Winner: Sean Myerson

31ST MAY 1999
Winner: Tom Archer

28TH MAY 2000
Winner: William Grundy

2001
No Single Wicket owing to foot-and-mouth

30TH JUNE 2002
Winner: Tom Archer

8TH JUNE 2003
Winner: Alistair Lloyd

23RD MAY 2004
Winner: Adam Macy

26TH JUNE 2005
Winner: Neil Carter

11TH JUNE 2006
Winner: Christopher Carter

2007
No Single Wicket Owing to Floods

8TH JUNE 2008
Winner: David Archer

25TH MAY 2009
Winner: Brenda Tucker

NIGEL'S JACKETS

Elizabeth frequently buys Nigel clothes as presents, including one year a jacket and matching waistcoat. For Christmas in 1993, she gave him a purple washed silk jacket, whilst in 2005 he unwrapped a very high-tech, waterproof and breathable new shooting jacket. Nigel has (of course) a waxed jacket and still owns (and wears) his grandfather's smoking jacket.

SUSAN GRUNDY'S SECRET RECIPE FOR SLOE GIN

Susan Grundy's secret was to prick each sloe twelve times *with a thorn from the same bush.* Be careful however not to drink the gin displaced from the bottle when inserting the pricked sloes or it becomes difficult both to aim the thorn and to remember how many times the sloe's been pricked…

MUCH-LOVED AMBRIDGE CANINES (1978)

DAN ARCHER
NELL, a sheepdog

JACK WOOLLEY
CAPTAIN, a Staffordshire Bull terrier

JOHN ARCHER
BESSIE, a mongrel Labrador/retriever cross puppy

GEORGE BARFORD
MEG, a gundog

EAT YOUR WAY ROUND AMBRIDGE: LOWER LOXLEY

When he worked as chef at Lower Loxley, one of Owen's specialities was lamb hotpot, whilst current Orangery chef Hugh's vanilla cheesecake is one of his best lines. Elizabeth doesn't like porridge and thinks a good breakfast should be bacon, eggs and mushrooms. She has to admit that Julia used to make a good risotto and also enjoys Nigel's special steak. Julia's sister Ellen once treated them all to her version of Albondigas en Salsa (meatballs in tomato sauce) when she was staying.

ON TOUR

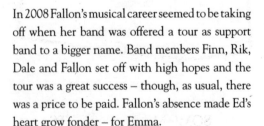

In 2008 Fallon's musical career seemed to be taking off when her band was offered a tour as support band to a bigger name. Band members Finn, Rik, Dale and Fallon set off with high hopes and the tour was a great success – though, as usual, there was a price to be paid. Fallon's absence made Ed's heart grow fonder – for Emma.

As she was about to leave, Ed gave Fallon a T-shirt with all the tour dates on the back – Colchester, Portsmouth, Brighton, Bristol, Felpersham, Birmingham, Manchester and Leeds, then Scotland – Paisley, St Andrews, Dundee.

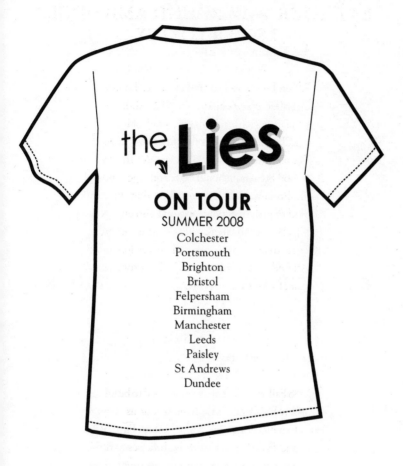

the **Lies**

ON TOUR
SUMMER 2008
Colchester
Portsmouth
Brighton
Bristol
Felpersham
Birmingham
Manchester
Leeds
Paisley
St Andrews
Dundee

SOME MORE T-SHIRTS
TO LOOK OUT FOR IN AMBRIDGE:

- Shires Bitter T-shirts
- Roy in his Aston Villa T-shirt
- David's 'designer-label' T-shirt – a Father's Day present
- Tom's yellow promotional T-shirts

And, rather more doubtful:

❧ William wearing the T-shirt which Emma gave him in 2004 with their photo printed on it (though possibly demoted for use as a wiping rag now?)

And, even further afield:

❧ Does Sam Batten still wear the T-shirt which Ruth and David bought him for his birthday (chosen by Pip)? It sports the slogan 'Not One of the Herd'.

EAT YOUR WAY ROUND AMBRIDGE: HOT STUFF

In her brief incarnation as a journalist on the *Borchester Echo*, Elizabeth was the unlikely author of a cookery column. Jill showed her how to make chilli, but when Elizabeth tried a solo dummy run only succeeded in making a mess of the kitchen. Further carelessness resulted in a misprint in the text, with the advice to use two tablespoons, rather than teaspoons, of chilli powder. Clarrie followed the recipe and nearly gave Eddie a seizure. When Elizabeth was subsequently sacked from the column, she naturally blamed Jill. Who was it who said 'a mother's place is in the wrong'?

SOME HORSES AT THE STABLES

- Marcie
- Maxwell
- Fleur
- Minty
- Colfax
- Pluto
- Sylvester
- Nimrod
- Silver
- Cottonwood
- Niobe
- Magnet
- Duff

People

The Archers Family Tree

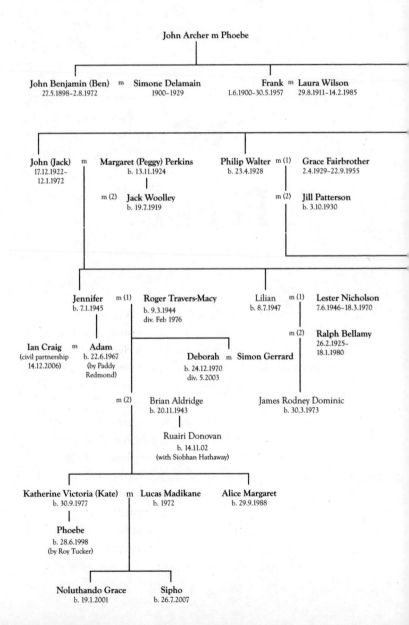

John Archer m Phoebe

John Benjamin (Ben) m **Simone Delamain**
27.5.1898–2.8.1972   1900–1929

Frank m **Laura Wilson**
1.6.1900–30.5.1957   29.8.1911–14.2.1985

John (Jack) m **Margaret (Peggy) Perkins**
17.12.1922–   b. 13.11.1924
12.1.1972

m (2) **Jack Woolley**
b. 19.7.1919

Philip Walter m (1) **Grace Fairbrother**
b. 23.4.1928   2.4.1929–22.9.1955

m (2) **Jill Patterson**
b. 3.10.1930

Jennifer m (1) **Roger Travers-Macy**
b. 7.1.1945   b. 9.3.1944
                     div. Feb 1976

Lilian m (1) **Lester Nicholson**
b. 8.7.1947   7.6.1946–18.3.1970

m (2) **Ralph Bellamy**
26.2.1925–
18.1.1980

Ian Craig m **Adam**
(civil partnership   b. 22.6.1967
14.12.2006)   (by Paddy
                     Redmond)

Deborah m **Simon Gerrard**
b. 24.12.1970
div. 5.2003

m (2) **Brian Aldridge**
b. 20.11.1943

James Rodney Dominic
b. 30.3.1973

Ruairi Donovan
b. 14.11.02
(with Siobhan Hathaway)

Katherine Victoria (Kate) m **Lucas Madikane**
b. 30.9.1977   b. 1972

Alice Margaret
b. 29.9.1988

Phoebe
b. 28.6.1998
(by Roy Tucker)

Noluthando Grace   **Sipho**
b. 19.1.2001   b. 26.7.2007

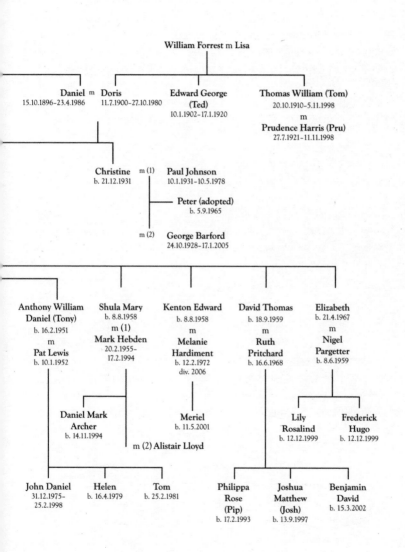

SOME AMBRIDGE RESIDENTS (1952)

Dan and Doris Archer
Christine Archer
Phil Archer
Jack and Peggy Archer
Angus and Jennie
Joe Blower
Simon and Bess Cooper
Admiral Bellamy
Benson
Miss Blowdon
Fred Bond
Mrs Brodie
Tom Browning
Tom Burroughs
Mr Beaumont
Elsie Catcher
Mrs Clark
Mrs Conway
Jim Cornford
Bill Churchman
Mike Daly
Doctor
Mr Emery
Mr Everton
Mr Fairbrother and Grace
Tom Forrest
Miss Finney
Colonel Fitzwilliam
Major Forbes
Walter and Nelson Gabriel
Harry Godwin
Mrs Goodby

Mr Garstand
Mr Hackett
Bill Hadley
Ken Hardwicke
Mr Hatherley
Fred Johnson
Tom Marney
Mrs Martin
Mrs Morgan
Mrs Murphy
Bob and Molly Oakley
Mr Parker
Mrs Perkins
Fred Pretty
Jim and Mrs Price
John Ridley (Vicar)
Mrs Racket
George Randall (P.C.)
Squire and Mrs Lawson-Hope
Sam
Fred Sparrow
Terry
Miss Thorpe
Mr Turnbull
Mr Vesty
Vet – Mr Wise
Fred Williams
Reuben Waikes
Mrs Weatherby
Ben White
Mrs Wragg

SWEEPING STATEMENT

Bert and Freda bought their Ewbank sweeper together
when Argos first opened in Felpersham.

COUNTRY NOUS

With a name like Zebedee Tring and his long-winded 'ooh-ar' delivery
of the simplest sentence, you might pigeonhole him as a slow-witted
countryman, but it was the ex-road-mender who correctly smelt a rat
rather than merely the waft of roast venison when the delicacy appeared
on the menu of the County Hotel in Borchester and a suddenly flush Joe
Grundy was found swigging malt whisky in the very same hotel's bar. As
Zebedee was anything but slow to point out, it was some coincidence
when two fallow deer had mysteriously vanished from Grey Gables
Country Park…

DOWN GRUNDY MEMORY LANE

- When William and Edward were little, Eddie was forever playing
  with their toys – William used to get upset because he could never
  get a go on his own Scalectrix.
- Joe remembers that when Eddie was small Susan knitted him a
  pair of mittens with 'L' and 'R' on them but he still got confused.
- When Clarrie and her sister Rosie were children, Whit Sunday
  marked the start of summer. They always had new clothes from top
  to toe.
- Susan cooked Joe his favourite meal every Saturday night for
  twenty-eight years.

- Joe's father used to have a Saddleback pig called Percy.
- Clarrie recalls that they had an Edam Cheese at Rosie's wedding: it was 'ever so posh' then.
- Ed's memories of Great Yarmouth, where he and Will raced on the dunes and used a pillbox as their 'castle', prompted him to hunt for Will there after their fight in 2008.
- There used to be a Kardomah café in Felpersham – Joe took Susan there once and they had pilchards on toast.
- Joe remembers Jethro and Walter telling him that they once had to use a hazel twig to stick a cow with a case of bloat. It was 'back in the days when farming was farming'.

CHEAP AS CHIPS

In their courting days Bert and Freda used
to enjoy a pennyworth of chips.

BERT'S FIFTEEN MINUTES
OF FAME

After Elizabeth, trying to shut him up, wrote an article for the *Borchester Echo* about his old country lore and rhyming couplets, Bert was invited to appear on the regional television show *In Your Corner*. The researcher, Alison Elliot, came to talk to him, and a dress rehearsal was held at Brookfield. Bert put on his best suit and a pink shirt but the presenter, Phyllida Johnston, suggested a more authentic look and gave him an apron to wear. Bert's fifteen minutes of fame only served to give him writers' block: his rhymes simply stopped flowing. Ruth suggested he should write about what he knew, and the Bard of Ambridge returned to form with a verse about his cat, Pickle.

YOU CAN TEACH AN OLD DOG NEW TRICKS

When they were first married, Phil's dog Timus was so clever at picking up the post that Jill hoped he'd be the first dog to learn to use a vacuum cleaner.

ROMEO JOE

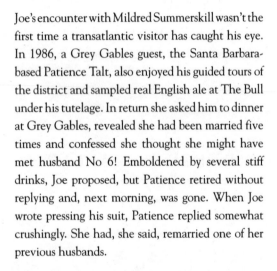

Joe's encounter with Mildred Summerskill wasn't the first time a transatlantic visitor has caught his eye. In 1986, a Grey Gables guest, the Santa Barbara-based Patience Talt, also enjoyed his guided tours of the district and sampled real English ale at The Bull under his tutelage. In return she asked him to dinner at Grey Gables, revealed she had been married five times and confessed she thought she might have met husband No 6! Emboldened by several stiff drinks, Joe proposed, but Patience retired without replying and, next morning, was gone. When Joe wrote pressing his suit, Patience replied somewhat crushingly. She had, she said, remarried one of her previous husbands.

SLITHERY ESCAPE

Jennifer gave milk recorder Libby Jones a silk evening shawl as a thank you for rushing Adam to hospital when he was bitten by an adder at the age of 11.

THE LIFE OF
MARJORIE ANTROBUS

Marjorie's husband Teddy served in the Colonial Service and she followed him willingly around the world. She learnt about beekeeping from her Arab neighbour in Palestine and noted that in Kenya, when one of the stockmen in the Mua Hills lost his house to a landslip, everyone in the village gave him something to replace his possessions. When Teddy was between postings he and Marjorie would stay with his mother, which was not easy for the young bride. Nor, however, was her arrival in Ambridge, at least as far as Tom Archer, then a toddler, was concerned. He was terrified of her Afghan hounds. Indeed, Marjorie herself could seem somewhat daunting, so it's hardly surprising to learn that she came from redoubtable female line, her aunt having been a suffragist.

BROOKFIELD HAPPY FAMILIES

- ❧ Jill has a photo of David as a small boy holding the bunch of freesias he had got her for Mothering Sunday.
- ❧ David used to celebrate every birthday by being sick.
- ❧ Elizabeth had a teddy bear called Frosty after 'Frosty

135

the Snowman'. Shula gave him to her for her sixth birthday.

- David used to squabble with Kenton and Shula over who got the biggest Christmas present.

- Jill thinks that Shula had Phil eating out of her hand when she was younger, because he was always giving in to her.

- David remembers building dams and fishing for tiddlers in the brooks around Midsummer Meadow.

- According to Kenton, David used to like wombats. As children they used to watch *Tinga and Tucker* on television.

- As a small child, Elizabeth used to spend hours looking at a Willow pattern plate and weaving every detail she could see on it into a story, such as a quest for magical treasure.

- Shula was mortified to be sent to school in a sweater knitted by her grandmother Doris. Everyone else had shop-bought V-necks.

- Kenton remembers running away with David when they were about eight following a telling-off from Jill. After purloining some food from the larder, they set off on their bikes for Penny Hassett but had only got just down the lane when they felt hungry. Pork pie and cheese and onion crisps on bread had, Kenton remembers, never tasted so good.

ILLNESSES AND AILMENTS (1950s)

- In early 1952, Peggy was admitted to Felpersham Isolation Hospital with diphtheria. It was a year before she was fully recovered.

- A year later, Nelson Gabriel, then serving with the RAF, fell ill and required a blood transfusion from his father, Walter.

- In the summer of 1954, Jack Archer had his first spell in the County Hospital for Nervous and Mental Disorders after a spell of erratic behaviour.

- Dan's brother Frank died in New Zealand, unleashing his rebarbative widow, Aunt Laura, on the village. Within weeks of her arrival she was diagnosed with mild heart trouble.

- In the summer of the same year, Doris started behaving mysteriously. She later revealed she had got to have all her teeth out.

- Just months after her marriage to Tom in September 1958, Pru Forrest was diagnosed with a patch on her lung and was sent to a sanatorium for six months.

HOLY HORROR

Alice screamed throughout her christening:
Bruno Foster (Snatch Foster's son and later fostered
briefly by Oliver and Caroline) was angelic.

NIGEL ON THE COUCH

Nigel's memories of his childhood would have kept Freud occupied for hours, possibly years. He remembers that his grandmother used to prod his grandfather with her walking stick when she was annoyed with him, whilst Nigel's mother Julia used to dress up as Burlington Bertie and read him Grimm's fairy tales (though not necessarily at the same time). Poor

Nigel found Julia's 'Rumpelstiltskin' voice particularly evil, and it never failed to give him nightmares. He also recalls his mother intruding on the 'secret kingdom' which he and his sister Camilla constructed for themselves in the Lower Loxley woodland by summoning him down from his den in the trees. At school, things were no better. Nigel's music master's regular refrain was: 'Spare us the caterwauling, Pargetter, just mouthe it silently!'

ESSENTIAL FACTS: ARCHERS

1. Ruth's eternity ring, given to her by David, is engraved with the words 'Just remember that I love you.'

2. Kenton was given a telescope as a reward for working hard for his GCSEs.

3. Pip was a bridesmaid at Roy and Hayley's wedding.

4. On the night that Phil's first wife Grace died in a fire at the stables, Christine was playing badminton.

5. Shula has cellulite, Ruth hasn't.

6. In 1996, before she married Alistair, Shula and Daniel went on holiday to the Seychelles with her former in-laws, Bunty and Reg Hebden.

7. Peacock blue suits David.

8. Daniel helps out with Neil's pigs, an interest the family think he inherited from Phil.

9. Pip's friend Izzy has her belly button pierced.

10. Jill and Phil met Diana, a widow from Sidmouth, in San Francisco. They went to Yosemite together; she was very knowledgeable about trees.

NEIL CARTER'S DRUG DEN

Ed and Jazzer's abortive cannabis factory, Jazzer's unfortunate ketamine overdose and Ed's descent into drink and drugs post-Emma are fresh in the mind, but back in 1974 it was Neil Carter who had a brush with the law over illegal substances. Besotted with a girl called Sandy Miller and oblivious to warnings that she was Not A Good Thing, he found himself at a party at her flat which was raided by the police. Reefers were found in a bemused Neil's pocket, Sandy denied all knowledge and, when questioned, Neil nobly refused to implicate her. He was found guilty of possession, placed on probation and given a Community Service Order – which in part perhaps explains why, with Ed's record, Neil was initially so very hard-line about Ed's suitability as his daughter Emma's boyfriend.

IT'S A FAIR COP

In August 1985, Nigel claimed he'd got a job as Chief of Police in Kuwait and asked Elizabeth to accompany him to his new posting.

AN AMBRIDGE EDUCATION

➤ When Christine passed her School Certificate, Dan gave her a little bookcase and told her that he was proud to have a scholar for a daughter. It was destroyed in the fire at the stables.

- Eddie maintains that the only school trip he went on was to Coventry Cathedral. Janice Smith was sick on the coach.
- When she was 14, Lilian had a teacher called Miss Molyneaux who caught her smoking behind the bike shed.
- Lewis can remember that when he was 10 years old they locked Spotty Wishart in the satchel cupboard for the whole of double Latin.
- When Phil was at the village school, it didn't even have an inside toilet. It still didn't when David, Kenton and Shula went there.
- Julia was awarded a copy of *Palgrave's Golden Treasury* for her spelling.
- On his first day at school, Alistair thought that his parents had just dumped him.
- Emma remembers 'Passion Alley' round the back of the Tech block at Borchester Green.
- Shula once had to do Annabel Lewis's maths homework for a week.

GODPARENTS

Alice Aldridge	Shula and Mark Hebden
Ben Archer	Tim Hathaway, Elizabeth Pargetter, Alistair Lloyd
John Archer	Jill Archer, Haydn Evans, Gerry Goodway
Josh Archer	Richard Locke
Phil Archer	Walter Gabriel
Pip Archer	Shula Hebden Lloyd
James Bellamy	Tony Archer, John and Carol Tregorran
Ruairi Donovan	Elizabeth Archer

Bruno Foster	Eddie Grundy
George Grundy	Roy and Brenda Tucker, Kenton Archer
William Grundy	Caroline Sterling, Sid Perks, Neil Carter
Daniel Hebden Lloyd	Nigel and Elizabeth Pargetter, Johnny
	(Mark's friend from Birmingham)
Ann Tregorran	Jill Archer, Hugo Barnaby, Lady Isabel Lander
Abbie Tucker	Brenda Tucker, Will Grundy,
	Elizabeth Pargetter

MORNING SICKNESS SUFFERERS

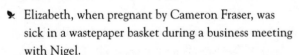

- Elizabeth, when pregnant by Cameron Fraser, was sick in a wastepaper basket during a business meeting with Nigel.
- Hayley suffered badly from morning sickness but found she could fancy porridge.
- When Sid's first wife Polly was expecting, she used to keep a packet of cream crackers by the bed so she could nibble one first thing in the morning.
- Sid's second wife Kathy, already ambivalent about her late baby, Jamie, suffered badly too.

CAROLINE STERLING'S DIARY FOR 1985

27 March	Hunt Ball – went with Nigel but seemed to spend all night dancing with Brian.
28 March	Brian phoned!!
4 April	Brian took me out to lunch and then for a long drive… Lovely afternoon.

5 April	He's asked me to go to London with him. Says we can stay at his friend Charles's flat... What to do? All very *Brief Encounter*, and exciting, but, but –
7 April	Brian's persuaded me – surprise, surprise. He says best we travel independently by train and meet up in London. Even more *Brief Encounter*.
9 April	To London.
11 April	Amazing time. Brian says now he has discovered my secret passion (Fortnum's apricots in brandy) he will buy them for me always.
21 April	Tony caught Brian and me together in the Country Park. Brian told him he was giving me a birthday kiss (was hardly that sort of kiss, but...), plus my birthday was on the 3rd. Tony not convinced.
24 April	Tony definitely suspicious. Keeps turning up at Grey Gables and hanging around as if I'm keeping Brian under the Reception desk or something.
25 April	Brian says I'm imagining things, Tony an idiot, etc., just carry on as we are.
28 April	Feel terrible about this.
1 May	Tony definitely following us – or me. Even popped up in the shop.
6 May	Tony turned up at the Mont Blanc where we were having lunch. Brian told him some story about how James (the manager) was my new boyfriend and I'd asked Brian along as independent critic of new menu. Even I didn't believe it. I have to finish this.
8 May	Awful, awful. Told Brian it's over. He won't listen.
10 May	Brian won't accept it.
15 May	Brian won't leave me alone. Told Mr Woolley got to have time off for family emergency – he's letting me go, bless him.
18 May	Brian has found out where I am and has been on phone, pleading. Says I have to go back to

	Ambridge. Told him I can't possibly, how can we both live in same village, what if Tony lets anything out, etc, etc.
26 May	Brian says I have to come back to Ambridge. If anyone should go, he says, it's him. Talking about selling up and moving Jennifer and the children to Devon!
1 June	Back in Ambridge. Brian and Jennifer going on holiday to Lanzarote.
6 June	Still so confused, talked to Shula. She was appalled – not just because of Jennifer but because she doesn't seem to see how attractive Brian is. Kept saying 'Brian?!?' Doesn't help. Anyway, it's over. Definitely.

And it was… until a couple of years later, when David's then girlfriend Sophie saw Brian, who was keen to rekindle things, with Caroline at an auction and mentioned it to Jennifer…

KEEPING YOUR OPTIONS OPEN

In the 1980s, Nigel always sent Valentine cards to
Shula, Elizabeth – and Jill.

AMBRIDGE AT WAR

Several older Ambridge residents have vivid memories of the Second
World War:

- During the war the local Ambridge policeman was called Jenkins.
- Joe served with the Home Guard, as did Tom Forrest and Walter.

❧ One night, out looking for German parachutists, Joe got so cold that he lost all feeling in his fingers and toes. When he got home, his mother packed him off to bed with no less than four hot water bottles.

❧ When Jack Archer first brought Peggy to visit Brookfield she couldn't believe the luxury of an egg for breakfast every morning. Doris packed her a big basket of provisions to take back to London. It included butter.

❧ Peggy had a friend called Kathleen who was killed in the Blitz. Her body was never found.

❧ Ambridge went short of sugar during the war but they could get most other things from the farms.

❧ When Walter was in the Home Guard, he took fright at Joe Blower's scarecrow and shot it to pieces.

❧ Jack Woolley was a fire warden in Stirchley. He was deemed unfit for the Army owing to a bad chest.

❧ Jack still has a copy of a Birmingham newspaper dated 12 April 1941. The front-page story relates that on the morning before the Germans dropped bombs over the city, the Bishop had a premonition and ordered the Burne-Jones window in the cathedral to be taken down. After the air raid, there wasn't a window left in St Martin's-in-the-Bullring; the only window saved was the Burne-Jones. Jack was one of the fire wardens who helped clear up, which is why he kept the paper.

THE HAPPIEST DAYS OF YOUR LIFE

❧ Susan's brother Clive Horrobin used to love Superman comics and films. One Christmas Susan saved up and bought him a Superman costume.

❧ Neil liked puppet shows like *Joe 90*.

- Brenda used to hold Mike's hand really tightly when they got near the old, gnarled tree beside the Am because she thought it looked like a witch and might come to life and get her.
- Debbie can remember Jennifer singing Beatles songs to her.
- Clarrie and her sister Rosie used to make dolls by bending the petals of poppies back and tying them round the middle with a blade of grass.
- At the age of 6, Tom preferred wearing a pair of Helen's pants to his own. They had pink dragons on them. He refused to give them back for months.
- Shula used to cut carrots into the shape of goldfish to get Daniel to eat them. When his friend Harry came to tea he burst into tears because he had a pet goldfish.
- When William Grundy didn't seem to enjoy school, Clarrie came to the conclusion that he was being bullied but discovered to her horror that it was William who was doing the bullying.
- Adam and Debbie used to play hide and seek at Home Farm but Debbie was always too scared to look in the cellar.

AN ACCIDENT WAITING TO HAPPEN (1950s)

Over the years, Ambridge residents have got themselves into some dreadful scrapes:

- Trying to convince Grace Fairbrother that he wasn't interested in Jane Maxwell, a young woman he'd recently employed to look after the poultry, Phil impulsively leapt onto the running board of Grace's car and knocked himself out on an overhanging branch.
- In the summer of 1951, Dick Raymond, Keith Latimer and Phil fought would-be ironstone saboteurs but escaped serious injury.
- Later the same year, Mrs P's nephew Bill Slater was less lucky

when he got into a fight outside The Bull and hit his head on a stone water-trough. He died in his sleep the following night.

- A year later, investigating a stalled tractor, Phil hit his head on the exhaust and damaged his eyesight. It required an operation to correct it.
- Tom Forrest was hurt in a fight with a poacher.
- Carol Grey arrived in the village in early 1954 and made her mark by immediately knocking John Tregorran off his scooter. In the same year, John was also attacked by gypsies.
- In February 1955, Christine broke her collarbone riding a temperamental horse belonging to Reggie Trentham.
- In September the same year, Grace, Phil's wife of just five months, died in a fire at the stables.
- Not two years later, Tom Forrest was arraigned on a manslaughter charge for shooting Ned Larkin's brother, Bob, whom he'd caught poaching.
- Skating on the village pond in January 1958, Lilian fell through the ice and had to be rescued by her father and Ned Larkin.
- Later that year, a newspaper report intimated that the boat on which Carol Grey was enjoying a sailing holiday had capsized off the Danish coast. It proved to be a false alarm.
- Dan ended the 1950s with a terrible run of luck. He fell off a roof he was repairing onto the binder and broke his leg, then slipped off his crutches in the dairy, resulting in suspected pneumothorax from a fractured rib.

ESSENTIAL FACTS: HOME FARM

1. As a child Adam was bitten by an adder.
2. He uses a quad bike for getting round the deer and the ewes.
3. Adam and Ian have a hot tub in the garden at Honeysuckle Cottage.

4. Ian runs a tidy kitchen but is a total slob at home.
5. Adam makes a good cup of tea.
6. Before her divorce from Simon Gerrard, Debbie wanted a baby.
7. She is now living with fellow farm manager Marshall Latham in Hungary. He originally comes from Hitchin and is not from a farming background.
8. Kate's daughter Nolly has a dog which she got as a puppy one Christmas.
9. Alice is studying Aeronautical Engineering at Southampton University.
10. She spent part of her gap year visiting Kate in South Africa and visited the AIDS orphanage where Kate works.

ELIZABETH'S BIRTHDAY BLUES

Elizabeth missed out on a big 18th birthday party and, unable to wait for her 21st, arranged a lavish bash for her 19th birthday in April 1986. The evening had to be cancelled, however, when her grandfather Dan died unexpectedly and when the guests were finally reconvened on 24th May she was in for a further disappointment. Having gone to much trouble to come up with a black and gold theme and to book a live band, The LeLulus, her then beau Tim Beecham flirted outrageously with YoYo, the lead singer, who encouraged him (not that he needed it) to pour cream all down her back.

THE LIFE OF MAURICE HORTON

Tom's butcher Maurice also works part-time at the supermarket on the retail park in Felpersham, but fits this around his hours for Tom. Maurice used to have his own business – a 'lovely little shop' according to him, but lost it as a result of his gambling. His wife also left him, along with their son. Maurice's last bet was over ten years ago but, with Alistair, he still attends Gamblers Anonymous. Maurice spoke up for Eddie when Eddie was accused of dealing in illegal meat and saved him from prosecution. He also showed his sensitive side in sympathising with Tom when Jack Woolley had to go into temporary nursing care. Maurice recalled that once his Granny Cora died, his grandfather shrank away to nothing. He went into a home and Maurice used to hate visiting him there.

LEADERS OF THE PACK

- Sid used to have an old Triumph motorbike that was a real bone-shaker.
- Neil Carter bought a second-hand motorbike with an endowment he received on his 18th birthday.
- Alan Franks is often seen zipping about the lanes between parishes on his trusty motorbike.
- Graham Collard, the Brookfield cowman in the 1980s, came off his motorbike one winter on a patch of ice and broke his leg.
- When Vladimir (Vlad), one of the farm managers in Hungary, had an accident on his motorbike, Debbie had to fly back early, cutting short one of her all-too-infrequent visits to Ambridge.
- Phil rode a motorbike in the 1950s; his scarf was described as 'streaming out behind him' on it.
- Roy thought of selling one of their cars and getting a motorbike to get to work when he and Hayley were considering taking on a big mortgage.
- The Lenten appeal in 2003 raised money for Motorbike Missionaries in Africa.

A LEVEL ANGST

Elizabeth has eight O levels – more than David – but only got an average of 36 per cent in her mock A levels, something which Phil attributed to the fact that she had by this time started going out with Nigel.

STAR-CROSS'D

In the 1970s and 1980s, it was Caroline who was Ambridge's Unluckiest in Love but these days the title would be shared between Fallon and Kirsty. Though neither is short of admirers who keep The Bull's tills ringing, Fallon's fling with Tom faltered when she found herself lugging display boards on a sausage promotion, and her promising romance with Ed fell apart when he went back to Emma. Kirsty, having been two-timed by Tom, found consolation with Hungarian worker Chaba – until he returned home and into the arms of his old girlfriend. Her romance with Brookfield herdsman Sam Batten also came to a bad end when he fell for Ruth.

LYNDA'S FENG SHUI OBSESSION

Lynda's interest in this Oriental aesthetic began in 2000 when her hay fever was worse than usual and she sought to introduce more positive energy to life at Ambridge Hall.

Her first action was to sand down the front door, as 'sticky doors indicate tension in a relationship'. She then removed Robert's Turkish rug from the hall, saying it was 'too brown'. Robert, peeved, was scornful of her Wealth Creation kit which she had bought at no small cost online, but found the Wealth Corner duly created useful when he needed small change for the car park. Lynda was livid: the three £1 coins he'd taken were especially lucky ones with Welsh dragons on them.

There was no rest for the poor man. Obeying a night-time call of nature, he banged his knee on the pot of the weeping fig which Lynda had installed in the bedroom, then had to confess to an unfortunate accident. He'd forgotten that the loo seat was now kept down. Worse was to follow when he broke a mirror which had been dispersing negative energy on the terrace. Lynda installed wind chimes but felt these didn't do the job as well. She finally solved the patio problem by getting a perplexed Eddie to re-lay it so as to provide a clear passage for the Ch'i across it and into the house through the conservatory.

Moving on from her successes at home (though Robert might disagree), Lynda offered her newly acquired skills to Jennifer at Home Farm. Brian was incensed to find a fuchsia installed outside his study window and demanded it be removed. Caroline, too, was less than receptive to Lynda's ideas at Grey Gables when the latter had the bed moved in Room 11 and a mirror removed from Room 16.

FRENCH CONNECTION

Christine and Paul Johnson nearly adopted a French baby before adopting Peter in 1965.

WOULD YOU WORK FOR BRIAN ALDRIDGE?

There seem to be no problems – as yet – with Brian's two current workers, Andy and Jeff, but his past record as an employer isn't that impressive.

JACK ROBERTS

Admittedly less worker than shirker, Brian sacked Roberts over a mix-up in the grain store in 1978 but, when challenged, then made the mistake of lashing out at him. Union rep Mike Tucker was hot on the case and, though neither assault nor unfair dismissal was proven, an industrial tribunal ruled, to Brian's annoyance, that Roberts could stay on in his cottage until he found another job.

BILL KNOWLES

There was slightly more justice in Brian's sacking of farm foreman Bill Knowles in 1990. Ruth, then on placement at Home Farm, had alerted him to the fact that Knowles had his nose in the supply reps' trough, and Brian was consequently paying over the odds for fertiliser.

STEVE OAKLEY

When Brian found out that farm worker Steve hadn't merely buried some drums of the newly banned herbicide DNBP as requested, but instead tipped off the Health and Safety Executive, who duly came to investigate, a row ensued. Debbie, who was going out with Steve, was caught in the middle. Sensibly realising he'd blown things with both his boss and his girlfriend, Steve returned to his home county of Shropshire.

SAMMY WHIPPLE

Despite Brian seeing him as something of a malingerer, Sammy survived as shepherd at Home Farm for 22 years until 1998, when Brian, wanting Sammy's cottage for his new gamekeeper Greg Turner, tried to make him redundant. Usha fought and won Sammy's case, giving him the right to stay put, but a £15,000 sweetener from Brian changed Sammy's mind. He and his wife moved to Felpersham.

ILLNESSES AND AILMENTS (1960s)

❧ Christine's husband Paul caught chicken pox.

❧ Phil, on a business trip to Holland with his boss Charles Grenville, was hospitalised with an infected foot.

❧ Reggie and Valerie Trentham's daughter Hazel (later to become Hazel Woolley) contracted a mild form of polio.

❧ Peggy had to make a mercy dash to London when her mother, Mrs P, fell ill.

❧ John Tregorran took a long sojourn in Spain to get over the death of his wife but ended up in hospital with a throat complaint.

❧ Frank Mead, father of Polly (later Polly Perks) was admitted to a mental hospital because he'd been setting fires all around the district.

❧ Phil and Jill's newborn baby, Elizabeth, had to have an operation to widen the pulmonary valve of her heart.

❧ Jack Archer, who had gambling debts, was found unconscious in bed nursing an empty whisky bottle.

❧ Lester Nicholson ('Nick'), Lilian's new boyfriend, was invalided out of the Canadian Air Force with ear trouble.

PARTY ANIMAL NIGEL

Having sworn that his daughters were having nothing more to do with 'that Nigel Pargetter' after Nigel, mistaking Phil and Jill's room for Shula's, had fumbled his way into bed with them, soft-hearted Phil nonetheless found himself renting Woodbine Cottage to Nigel. The house-warming was typically riotous: Tim Beecham tried to rip down The Bull's pub sign, Mrs Potter's garden gnome was thrown into the village pond, David drunkenly crashed out in a hammock and the Lawson-Hope seat found its way from the Green to Lakey Hill. To this day no one remembers quite how.

ESSENTIAL FACTS: THE GRUNDYS

1. The landlord at The Goat and Nightgown in Borchester is an old friend of Eddie's.
2. George has a toy tractor Ed bought him for his birthday.
3. Alf Grundy, Joe's elder son, lives in Gloucester. Joe visited him at Christmas 2008. It was not a success.
4. Eddie's friend Fat Paul's wife goes to church in Darrington.
5. Clarrie's favourite cake is ginger.
6. Eddie's friend Baggy drinks in The Dragon.
7. Joe has false teeth.
8. George calls Clarrie 'Grandma'.
9. Ed was named Edward after Prince Edward as much as after his father. He was born on a Friday – 'loving and giving'.
10. William inherited George Barford's gun. George is named after George Barford, who was Christine's husband.

BAPTISMAL NAMES IN FULL

Peggy	Margaret Beryl Perkins
Phil	Philip Walter Archer
George	George Randall Barford
Tony	Anthony William Daniel Archer
Kenton	Kenton Edward Archer
Shula	Shula Mary Archer
David	David Thomas Archer
James	James Rodney Dominic Bellamy
Oliver	Oliver Peregrine Sterling
Nigel	Nigel Gerald Pargetter

Kate	Katherine Victoria Aldridge
Alice	Alice Margaret Aldridge
John	John Daniel Archer
Pip	Philippa Rose Archer
Josh	Joshua Matthew Archer
Ben	Benjamin David Archer
Daniel	Daniel Mark Archer Hebden (now Hebden Lloyd)
Lily	Lily Rosalind Pargetter
Freddie	Frederick Hugo Pargetter
George	George Edward Grundy
Abbie	Abigail Elizabeth Tucker

A SHAGGY DOG STORY

In 1984, Caroline acquired a 6-month-old pedigree Old English Sheepdog known as Charlie. His full name was Charlton Peregrine the Third. How odd that she was later to marry a Peregrine – it's Oliver's middle name.

EARTH MOTHER

Jennifer's first grandchild was born in June 1998 in a tent at the Glastonbury Festival, with the help of handily placed midwife Morwenna, but fears that her wild-child mother Kate Aldridge would name the baby 'Rainbow' or 'Summer' were unfounded. In a naming ceremony on Lakey Hill, Kate named her baby after her own great-great-grandmother on the Archer side, Phoebe. Kate gave a similar nod to Archer family tradition when she gave her second daughter, known as Nolly, the full name of Noluthando Grace.

THE AMBRIDGE (B)RAT PACK

Gary Kenton, Ricky Boyd, 'Dusty' Rhodes and Jimmy Grange – no, not the members of a boy band but the bad lads of Ambridge in the late 1950s and early 1960s. Gary ran his own chicken enterprise and Jimmy was Dan Archer's apprentice, but Ricky was a layabout who ended up in prison, while light-fingered Dusty filched the Youth Club Funds. A spell on probation obviously taught him nothing, as, turning on poor Jimmy, a talented skiffle player, he threw a brick through his guitar. There are other ways of showing someone you don't like their sounds.

BRUSHES WITH DRUGS

- In 2002, Alistair's partner Theo was revealed as a cocaine addict.
- Kate Aldridge was seen by a shocked William and Brenda smoking dope on the village green in 1995.
- Kate later served her parents a cannabis casserole, which put them in a very 'relaxed' mood.
- Ed and Jazzer cultivated cannabis in a barn at Bridge Farm until discovered by Tony.
- Alan was distraught at his inability to help drug addict Luke, who he even took in to live at the vicarage.

SEWING SAINT

Dan Archer is always thought of as a virtual saint, but when he ordered a new sewing machine for Doris in 1972 he wasn't above asking the supplier to make out an invoice for 'farm equipment'.

AN ACTOR'S LIFE

Scott Daniels was Lilian's actor boyfriend,
a good twenty years her junior.

CURRICULUM VITAE: SCOTT DANIELS

TV
The Bill
Customer in a bank raid
ITV

FILM
Pendre la cremaille ('Housewarming')
Medieval French Knight
European art house distribution only; DVD available

AGE RANGE
18 – 38

SKILLS
Motorbike licence

ACTING MOTTO
'Put on the clothes and you find the man'

DATING DISASTERS

The course of true love has tended not to run
smoothly for Ambridge residents who've tried
'Lonely Hearts' ads or the like:

JOE

When lonely Joe advertised himself as a 'gentleman farmer' in the *Borchester Echo*, he attracted the attentions of none other than Marjorie Antrobus, followed by a few promising dates with Sandra. Sadly, when it emerged that he was only a tenant farmer, any possible romance withered away.

CAROLINE

Caroline tried dating in 1997, after the death of her first husband Guy. There was much interest but a string of disasters began when her first date turned out to be Lynda's thespian rival, Larry Lovell. The second wore a wig and the third was coin dealer Doug, who spent the whole evening talking about his ex-wife. Finally, her dream date arrived – tall, dark, handsome, cultured – and married (of course). Then it was back to earth, first with Graham Ryder and next with Mr Cash, a banker who was such a bore that Nigel had to rescue her by pretending to be her husband.

KATHY

Realising after her divorce that her choice of available men in Ambridge was limited to Jean-Paul, Higgs, Joe Grundy or Eddie's friend Fat Paul, Kathy tried a Singles dinner party where she met a seemingly promising man, Richard. On their date, however, she discovered that he had not one but two fatal flaws. Not only did he collect menus, hence his interest in the dinner parties, but was a world authority on staplers, which he sold for a living.

MIKE

Too modest to 'sex up' his advert, Mike's take-me-as-I-am ad elicited two replies, whilst Hayley's more romanticised version garnered four. Mike arranged to meet 'Wendy' from his ad and 'Corinne' from Hayley's – only to discover that they were one and the same person. He managed a further few dates with Wendy, but their relationship fizzled out when she took him to the theatre. Unable to understand the fuss in *The Cherry Orchard* ('if the trees were that old, they'd never have been cropping properly anyway'), he thought the interval was curtain down. Wendy told him that she didn't think it was working out. Mike has now been swept off his (dancing) feet by Vicky.

BORCHESTER LAND
COMMITTEE MEMBERS

Brian Aldridge (Chair)
Gerry Moreton
Andrew Eagleton
Andrew Smith
Annabelle Schrivener
Martyn Gibson

Stephen Chalkman was voted off the board in his
absence and Matt Crawford removed as Chairman in April 2009.
Matt resigned from the Board the following month.

WALTER AND DORIS

Though his farming methods exasperated them both, Walter was a frequent guest of Dan and Doris at Brookfield, especially if there was food on the go or if (as was common since his cottage was so badly maintained) he needed a roof over his head while repairs were carried out. After a series of disasters, Doris was heard to say plaintively she could cope with Walter staying 'as long as he doesn't try to help me'. This, though, was something Walter never ceased trying to do…

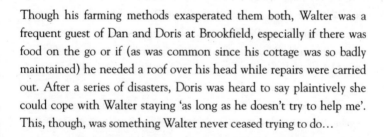

- Walter was fascinated when Doris's formerly hand-turned
  sewing machine was converted to work 'off the electric'
  in 1952. Attempting to grease it for her, he spilt oil all
  over it.
- Though Doris was a notorious teetotaller, he got her
  tiddly (at the vicar's housewarming of all places) by
  plying her with elderflower wine.

- As Doris's houseguest once again in 1977, he scoured her saucepans, thinking they were burnt, and succeeded in removing their non-stick coating.
- Trying to be helpful and fix a wonky door handle, he replaced it the wrong way round so the door couldn't be opened at all.
- Doris had a wall clock which only worked if hung at a slight angle. Walter straightened it with the result that it stopped working. Time to go, perhaps!

THE NAME GAME

- Jolene is a stage name. She was christened Doreen.
- Fallon is named after one of the lead characters in the 1980s soap opera *Dynasty*.
- Bruno Foster, Snatch's son, was named after his dad's hero, boxer Frank Bruno.
- When he came to the village, Roger Travers-Macy was using the name Roger Patillo as a rebellion against his parents. He'd stayed at the Villa Patillo in the South of France as a child.
- Nelson Gabriel (surprisingly) was a real name, though Scotland Yard often wondered otherwise.
- 1950s Ambridge resident, thriller writer Mike Daly was not a writer at all but a secret service agent with daring wartime service behind him. He'd been given a new identity in the war as Major John Smith.
- He was spirited away from the village by Baroness Czorva, who had a mission for him which he chose to accept.
- Destiny was the hairdresser who did Emma's hair for her wedding as well as the name of a lap dancer at a club once visited by Kenton, Nigel and Matt.
- Nigel's mother Julia was christened Joan.

- Shula's ex-mother-in-law 'Bunty' Hebden's real name is Audrey.
- General Sir Borthwick 'Bunny' Hare escorted Marjorie Antrobus to an Ambridge barn dance in 1987.
- Madame Garonne, Charles Grenville's housekeeper in the late 1950s, was Denise to her (few) friends. No wonder she kept herself to herself: she was later exposed as a diamond smuggler.
- The real name of Eddie's one-time fiancée, flighty Dolly Treadgold, was Lesley.

ESSENTIAL FACTS: THE CARTERS

1. Emma has retained her cleaning duties at Brookfield on top of her new job at Lower Loxley, but Ivy Horrobin now cleans for Adam and Ian.
2. When Emma was born in August 1984 she was premature and very small.
3. In 1994 while Susan was in prison, Emma started wetting her bed.
4. Neil spent years blaming Ed for the accident that disfigured Emma's leg but is now reconciled to him.
5. Susan's brother Clive Horrobin was sentenced to twelve years in prison in 2004.
6. Christopher looks good without his shirt on.
7. George calls Susan 'Nanna'.
8. Christopher has a tattoo declaring his love for Alice. Susan does not approve of it, though she is very supportive of his relationship with Alice.
9. Neil is an orphan.
10. When Neil left his job as Brookfield's pigman, Phil gave him a computer.

NANNY KNOWS BEST

- Mrs Beard was employed by Lilian and Ralph Bellamy to look after the infant James. She lived in the nanny flat at The Dower House, later William Grundy's flat and now Matt Crawford's office.

- Dawn Porritt worked for Brian and Jennifer when Alice was born. Jack Woolley took a great shine to her.

- Previously, Brian and Jennifer had had a German au pair, Eva Lenz, to look after Kate. Eva married the Ambridge Policeman, PC Coverdale. They moved to Portsmouth in the mid 1980s.

- To get away from Ambridge and a relationship with John Archer which she didn't think was working out, Sharon Richards, Clive Horrobin's ex, moved to Leeds with her young daughter Kylie for a job as a live-in mother's help.

- Michele Gravencin, the au pair at Brookfield in the 1970s, was the target of gamekeeper Gordon Armstrong's amorous intentions, but had to leave the village when her mother fell ill.

- Nigel had a nanny who used to tell him that the stone gryphons at Lower Loxley would come to life and eat naughty children.

- George Grundy calls Clarrie 'Grandma' and Susan 'Nanna'.

AN ACCIDENT
WAITING TO HAPPEN (1960s)

- Doris cut her head badly when Walter crashed his bus.
- In March 1961, he knocked 16-year-old Jennifer off her bicycle. She broke her leg.
- Weeks later, Walter himself was left unconscious when he was attacked by vandals who'd torched a hay barn. Things could have got even nastier, but Estate owner Charles Grenville arrived and broke one of the hooligans' arms with a judo blow.

Walter's mishaps set the tone for the early 1960s:

- Eighteen months later, Jack Woolley broke his ankle and sprained his wrist in a car accident.
- Having moved to Newmarket in 1962 for Paul's work, Christine had a bad riding accident and Doris had to go and look after her.
- In October 1963, John Tregorran's new wife Janet, the passenger in Charles Grenville's car, was killed when it crashed. Grenville lost a leg. A little over a year later he too was dead, the result of a long-dormant bug he'd picked up in the Far East.
- Dan's bad luck continued in the 1960s when he slipped a disc trying to move a heavy tractor wheel.
- Nelson Gabriel was reported dead in a plane crash.
- Doris was knocked down the stairs and left for dead by an intruder at Brookfield. She broke her wrist and was left with memory lapses for months.
- Yet again, Dan was a magnet for disaster. Late in 1968, he jumped into the slurry pit to save a cow which had slipped in; another cow fell on top of him, injuring his shoulder.

UNREQUITED LOVE

- When he first arrived in the village, Neil had a crush on Shula.
- Eddie used to fancy his chances with Lilian.
- When Susan was in prison, lonely housewife Maureen ('call me Mo') Travis developed an unhealthy interest in Neil.
- The Archer family tried to marry off Phil to Carol Grey (later Grenville, and even later, Tregorran).
- Owen King aka Gareth Taylor thought he had 'a relationship' with Kathy.
- Elizabeth dallied with a business contact called Hugo.
- John Archer proposed to Hayley (now Tucker) the night before he died.
- Clarrie used to be deeply jealous of Eddie's relationship (to be fair, mostly professional) with Jolene.

THE LONGEST NAME IN AMBRIDGE

Tony (Anthony William Daniel Archer) was overtaken by Daniel (Daniel Mark Archer Hebden Lloyd) in 2000, when Daniel was formally adopted by his new stepdad, Alistair Lloyd.

MODERN LIVING

After fifteen years of shilly-shallying and each marrying someone else in the meantime, it still wasn't plain sailing when John Tregorran and Carol Grenville finally got together in 1967. First they had to decide which of their two houses (Blossom Hill Cottage and Manor Court) to live in; then John insisted to his independent (and wealthy) wife that he'd expect to be responsible for the household bills. Carol was having none of it, telling him she intended to teach him to 'move with the times'. So Pat wasn't the first feminist in Ambridge…

THE CAT AND FIDDLE

Joe and Eddie were crying into their beer when the friendly landlord of The Cat, Dickie Pearson, was replaced in 1983 by an ex-army man who had once run a boxing club in Leeds. Worse was to come. Unlike the previous laissez-faire regime, the new man kept strictly to opening hours, and when Eddie, showing off in front of his then mate Snatch Foster, spilt beer over a customer who happened to be a friend of the new landlord, he found himself picked up and ejected – by the seat of his pants.

LORDING IT

As he eased himself into his new role as country squire after his arrival in Ambridge in 1962, Jack Woolley tried to get into hunting and shooting, talking of buying a brace of Purdey shotguns at an eye-watering £1,000.

TEN TITBITS ABOUT JOE GRUNDY

- When Joe was a boy, nobody helped him with his homework. He left school when he was 14 and claims it never did him any harm.
- His wife Susan died suddenly in 1969. Joe put her

personal things in a tin box tied up with string and placed it in the hayloft at Grange Farm.

- Joe has a collection of Vera Lynn records but he can't sing.
- At night time, Joe won't use a duvet, he still sleeps under blankets.
- Joe still smokes: he buys his 'baccy' from the village shop.
- Joe loves steak and kidney pie.
- He has cut down his sugar to just one spoonful in tea.
- Joe has false teeth and can't eat muesli.
- He likes malt whisky.
- Joe takes a bath once a week whether he needs it or not.

NELSON'S WINE BAR

A visit to Nelson Gabriel's late-lamented Wine Bar in West Street was not for the faint-hearted. Walter's sophisticated son had strict ideas about the sort of customer he considered desirable and once made someone who had committed the sartorial crime of wearing a Crimplene trouser suit wait half an hour to be served. He also banned wellingtons and overalls.

Once past the dress code, however, the rewards were immense. The menu, on which 'Lisa's lettuce soup' and temperamental chef Shane's quiche were popular staples, was extensive. Mark Hebden's one-time girlfriend Jackie Woodstock, though, once dared to complain that there was too much crumble and not enough fruit in her raspberry and apple crumble. Shane's response is not known, but may have involved one of his spectacular flounces.

Christmas was always memorable for Shane's flamboyant decorations: one year the entire bar was swathed in tartan. There was also a special wine bar punch for the festive season.

ACCIDENT? SUICIDE?
OR A CRY FOR HELP?

Greg Turner, Brian's gamekeeper, shot himself in the shepherd's hut in the woods in May 2004. His ex-wife Michelle had turned truculent and, despite the loving support of his girlfriend Helen Archer, he felt a failure in every way, mostly as far as his two daughters were concerned.

George Barford, also a gamekeeper, and in similar despair about his broken marriage (to a staunch Catholic) and unsatisfactory contact with his children, took an overdose in 1974. He was found just in time by Tom and Pru Forrest.

A depressed 18-year-old Kate Aldridge saw in the New Year of 1996 with a mixture of whisky and temazepam (a thoughtful Christmas present from her then drug-dealer boyfriend Jolyon). Whether it was a serious attempt or a cry for help was something Jennifer, with her devotion to 'family therapy' was only too willing to try to tease out.

Even more ambiguous was Christine's first husband Paul Johnson's death in a car crash in Germany in 1978. Under pressure from the Archer family to return to the UK for a bankruptcy hearing, he died in an accident on the Autobahn. The coroner recorded a verdict of death by misadventure, but given that German cars are notoriously reliable…

ILLNESSES AND AILMENTS (1970s)

* Having returned to Ambridge following the death of her 'second Perkins', Mrs P began to suffer from dizzy spells. A diet was recommended.
* Doris was diagnosed with high blood pressure and went to hospital for tests and observation.

- Jack Archer's excesses finally took their toll and, after tests at Borchester General, he was moved to a sanatorium in Scotland where he died in January 1972.
- Dan started suffering with lumbago.
- Jill, suffering with nervous exhaustion, went to stay with a school friend for three months. On her return, she worried that Phil was suffering from overwork and strain after he crashed his car.
- Joe Grundy spent time in hospital with farmer's lung. When his doctor put him on a diet to get his weight down, he took it too seriously and collapsed from malnutrition outside The Bull.
- Farmer Haydn Evans slipped a disc. His niece Pat came to look after him and within weeks had proposed to Tony.
- Lilian's second husband Ralph was told he needed complete rest or he'd have a heart attack. He and Lilian promptly left Ambridge for Guernsey.
- Jill's mysterious tiredness was explained only after she collapsed and was rushed to hospital. It was a thyroid deficiency, myxoedema.
- Jethro developed gum trouble and had to have the rest of his teeth out.
- Pat had to return to Wales to look after her sick mother.
- Joe Grundy was found by Shula and Mary Pound delirious with flu.
- Neil was rushed to hospital suffering from Weil's disease, contracted when rats' urine entered his system via a cut hand.
- Martha Woodford was off work for weeks with pneumonia.
- Pat and Tony's daughter Helen was born with 'clicky hips'.
- Doris suffered ulcers under her dental plate.
- George Barford was an alcoholic.
- Sid collapsed with an ear infection.
- Walter was diagnosed with diabetes.

ESSENTIAL FACTS:
LYNDA AND ROBERT

1. When she first started writing for *Borsetshire Life*, Lynda used the name Dylan Nells.
2. Lynda is allergic to bee stings; she has a terrible reaction.
3. Lynda and Robert have B&B guests.
4. Lynda and Robert now own Scruff the dog, who used to belong to the Hebden Lloyds. Daniel still loves him and often goes to see him.
5. Lynda Feng Shui'd Ambridge Hall.
6. Lynda's lucky number is 7.
7. Robert Snell has a sweet tooth.
8. Robert's daughter Coriander got her name having been conceived after an especially good Indian meal.
9. Coriander and her partner Justin are now expecting a baby of their own.
10. Lynda's kitchen has granite work surfaces.

MODS

Scooter and moped riders have included:
Jennifer Archer
Christine Archer
Tony Archer
John Tregorran
Emma Grundy (through the 'Wheels to Work' scheme)
Kate Aldridge – desperate to get out of Ambridge
by any means possible in the 1990s

WASH THAT MAN...

In 1974, Martha Woodford tried to persuade her husband Joby that she needed a washing machine, but he wouldn't agree to her spending money on frivolities. When leaving wet washing deliberately dripping on his head from the ceiling airer failed to make her point, Martha, in an uncharacteristic display of independence, went ahead and bought herself a fully automatic machine anyway. She'd failed, however, to take account of the little matter of plumbing in, but Joby's smirks were wiped from his face when Neil, at that time their lodger, booked and paid for a plumber. Martha's smalls never looked back.

ALICE ALDRIDGE'S CIRCLE

FRIENDS

Amy Franks	Chloe	Holly
Venetia Streatfield	Rebecca	Daisy
India Beesborough	Davina	Caitlin

EX-BOYFRIENDS

Harry (when she was 15)	Damian
Dimitri (fruit picker)	Lajos (fruit picker)

RUAIRI'S MEMORY BOX

Ruairi's memory box was made by him for his mother, Siobhan, before her death in May 2007. It contains:

- Photographs
- Ruairi's Christening blanket
- Siobhan's crucifix
- A diary
- A shell Siobhan and Ruairi picked up on a beach
- His baby scans

For a Christening present, Brian gave Ruairi a fob watch which had belonged to his grandfather.

THE MADIKANE FAMILY TREE

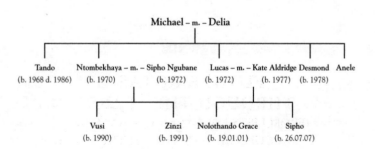

JOE GRUNDY'S SAMPLER

In pride of place in Joe Grundy's bedroom (along with his recliner chair) is his late wife Susan's sampler. It was made for her by her Auntie Vi.

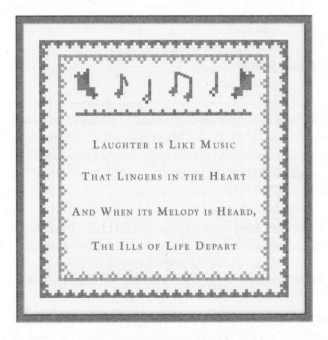

LAUGHTER IS LIKE MUSIC

THAT LINGERS IN THE HEART

AND WHEN ITS MELODY IS HEARD,

THE ILLS OF LIFE DEPART

FLOWER ROTAS
THROUGH THE YEARS
(FROM LISTS FOUND AT THE BACK OF
A CUPBOARD IN THE VESTRY)

JUNE 1955

First Sunday
Doris Archer; Grace Archer

AUGUST 1963

First Sunday
Jill Archer; Peggy Archer

Second Sunday
Carol Grey; Mme Denise Garonne

Third Sunday
Mrs Polly Perkins;
Mrs Helen Fairbrother

Fourth Sunday
Mrs Scroby; Mrs Agatha Turvey

Second Sunday
Janet Tregorran; Carol Grenville

Third Sunday
Doris Archer;
Laura Archer

Fourth Sunday
Jill Archer; Christine Johnson

SEPTEMBER 1975

First Sunday
Jill Archer; Carol Tregorran

Second Sunday
Lizzie Larkin;
Jennifer Travers-Macy

Third Sunday
Polly Perks; Laura Archer

Fourth Sunday
Doris Archer; Nora Salt

MAY 1985

First Sunday
Clarrie Grundy; Christine Barford

Second Sunday
Pat Fletcher;
Jean Harvey

Third Sunday
Laura Archer; Pru Forrest

Fourth Sunday
Peggy Archer; Jennifer Aldridge

JANUARY 1996

First Sunday
Marjorie Antrobus; Freda Fry

Second Sunday
Jill Archer; Shula Hebden

Third Sunday
Christine Barford; Lynda Snell

Fourth Sunday
Betty Tucker; Susan Carter
(Note: Mrs P. Woolley now resigned –
protest against female vicar –
DO NOT ASK!!)

SEPTEMBER 2008

First Sunday
Shula Hebden Lloyd; Lynda Snell

Second Sunday
Jill Archer; Jennifer Aldridge

Third Sunday
Susan Carter; Pat Fletcher

Fourth Sunday
Clarrie Grundy; Usha Franks

WALTER'S GRANNY'S SAYINGS: ONE FOR EVERY DAY OF THE WEEK

Walter Gabriel's Granny was a very shrewd old lady whose pearls of wisdom are as useful today as they were during her lifetime – or his for that matter. Here are a few worth remembering:

- 'Though shabbily clothed and untidily shod,
  A Gabriel will always look like a God.'
- 'Roll the baby in the snow and all its aches and pains will go.'
- 'A farmer who won't help a friend when he ought
  Will finish his days in the bankruptcy court.'
- 'Drink beer when you're thirsty, it's tastier and wetter,
  A half pint is good, but a pint is much better.'
- 'Come to the point and get there quick,
  Shilly-shallying makes me sick.'
- 'A girl who gets tied to a chap twice her age,
  Afore long she's just like a bird in a cage,
  She's fettered and prisoned and that's gospel truth,
  So let age keep to age and let youth stick to youth.'
- 'No matter how humble, how rough or how rude,
  A man should be willing to show gratitude.'

FLU JABS

The following people will all be over 65
in October 2009 and will have the flu jab:
Jill Archer
Phil Archer
Christine Barford

173

Joe Grundy
Bob Pullen
Robert Snell
Jack Woolley
Peggy Woolley

And for the first time (not good for his ego!):

Brian Aldridge

The jab is also given to those in contact with poultry
such as Neil, Hayley, Roy, Eddie, Clarrie and Will,
owing to the threat of a mutation with bird flu.

THE VILLAGE PUMP

Uncle Tom (Forrest) – Phil's mother Doris's brother – used to sing at
every village occasion. His favourite party piece was a special Ambridge
version of a popular song, 'The Village Pump':

There's a pretty little village far away,
Where they grows new potatoes, corn and hay,
There's a tricklin' little rill,
That works a little mill,
And a mill it keeps a-workin' all the day.
There's a lot of little 'ouses in the middle,
And two pubs, The Bull and Cat and Fiddle,
But you make no mistake,
The thing that takes the cake,
Is the pride of all the place, the Village Pump.

❋

The Village Pump, The Village Pump,
The Village Pump, Pump, Pump, Pump, Pump.
The Village Pump, The Village Pump,
The Village Pump, Pump, Pump, Pump, Pump.

❀

One night the rummest chap you've ever seen,
Gave a temperance lecture on the village green.
He said us fellows here
Was much too fond of beer,
And he spouted like a penny magazine.
He damned The Cat and Fiddle and The Bull,
Till Jethro aimed a clout across his skull,
He said 'Water – that's for me!'
So we shouted, 'Right you be!'
And we took him out and ducked him in the pump.

❀

The Village Pump, The Village Pump,
The Village Pump, Pump, Pump, Pump, Pump.
The Village Pump, The Village Pump,
The Village Pump, Pump, Pump, Pump, Pump.

ESSENTIAL FACTS:
THE CHURCH/ALAN AND USHA

1. The new Bishop of Felpersham who replaced Bishop Cyril is called 'Bishop Andrew'.
2. Until recently, the only time Alan did any gardening at The Vicarage was when Mabel forced him to.
3. Usha's brother Shiv is a bit of a gourmet.
4. The Archdeacon is Rachel Dorsey.

5. Usha plays poker. Alan once gave her a book of poker techniques.
6. Before Alan and Amy moved into Ambridge, the vicarage was the surgery and was only used as business premises.
7. Celia is the Sunday school teacher in Darrington.
8. After the church was burgled in 2004, a new Bishop's Chair and lectern were commissioned in a contemporary design.
9. Alan is good looking: his eyes are so blue you could get lost in them.
10. There's a statue of Shiva in the living room at the Vicarage.

SHHH!

Shula seriously considered becoming a librarian.

FURTHER EDUCATION

Freda Fry	Flower arranging
Susan	Cake decorating (in prison in 1994)
Lynda	Feng shui; aromatherapy ('Essentially Yours')
Jennifer	Weaving (in the 1970s, to use Jacob's sheep wool)
Brenda	American literature (her tutor was Debbie's then husband, Simon Gerrard)
Oliver and Caroline	Italian, so they could pursue their interest in opera (Caroline feared Oliver was more interested in pursuing their tutor, Cosima)
Jill	French
Pat	Women's Studies (in the early 1980s, with friend Rose); Tai Chi (in 2004, with Betty Tucker)
Polly Perks	Hairdressing (the tutor, Monsieur Phillippe, was found to be a fraud)

| Elizabeth | Marketing |
| Ruth and Usha | Salsa dancing (including a couple of less successful sessions where they dragged David and Alan along) |

NEARLY TWENTY YEARS OF GRUNDY TURKEY TRAUMAS

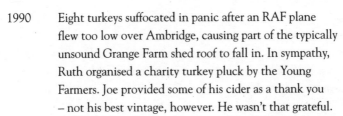

1990   Eight turkeys suffocated in panic after an RAF plane flew too low over Ambridge, causing part of the typically unsound Grange Farm shed roof to fall in. In sympathy, Ruth organised a charity turkey pluck by the Young Farmers. Joe provided some of his cider as a thank you – not his best vintage, however. He wasn't that grateful.

1998   Bothered by feather-pecking, Joe's cure involved stringing up cabbages for the turkeys to peck at instead – a tip from his old dad.

1999   15-year-old Ed and 11-year-old Christopher (easily led) foolishly frightened some of the Grange Farm turkeys to death by letting off fireworks in their shed.

2001   In a munificent gesture, Lynda offered her shed for the turkey-gutting. To her chagrin, guests arriving for her pre-Christmas party preferred watching this charming country tradition to mingling and nibbling canapés.

2002   By now living at Keeper's Cottage, Joe made a pet of a turkey which he called Bathsheba. Sentiment didn't stop him enjoying her for Christmas lunch.

2003   Eddie improved the customarily freezing plucking conditions in the Grundys' Field shed by installing a paraffin heater, but, sickened by the smell of feathers as they landed on it and burnt, Clarrie instead tried to keep warm by being hung about with hot water bottles.

2004   In this year, poor Clarrie's turkey-plucking conditions
        were made worse by having to share the shed with Eddie's
        leering garden gnomes.

2008   Joe was delighted when William, at first reluctant, said he'd
        come back from Gloucester to help with the annual turkey
        pluck. Joe regards it as a family ritual.

POETIC JUSTICE

Ambridge almost got its own literary giant when a yellowed poem turned up under the binding of an old book. Thrillingly, the little-known nineteenth-century poet Josiah Goodall had apparently been married to an Ambridge woman, Tabitha Thorncroft. Knowing he'd ended up being deported, Lynda found out he'd been not only a poet but, even better, an agricultural reformer – obviously a hero! Only then did she discover that he was in fact a bigamist who'd been in and out of prison all his life. Not then the kind of connection that Ambridge would want to advertise…

THE LIFE OF JETHRO LARKIN

Jethro was Clarrie's dad and Brookfield's farm worker. One of the old school, he always called Phil 'Master Phil' or 'Boss' and David 'Master David' and, when surprised, would exclaim, 'My eye!' Following the example of the French Foreign Legion, Jethro used to wear his hanky under his cap in the summer to protect the back of his neck. When Jethro and Neil worked together at Brookfield in the 1980s, they regularly munched their lunchtime sandwiches in the tractor shed, but Jethro was no gourmet. When Clarrie went to visit her sister Rosie in Great Yarmouth, leaving Joe and Eddie to fend for themselves, they congratulated themselves on being asked to Jethro's for Sunday lunch. To their disgust, however, the meal was a tiny half-shoulder of lamb and a tin of mandarin oranges with evaporated milk. Jethro sadly died in a tragic farm accident at Brookfield in June 1987.

AN ACCIDENT
WAITING TO HAPPEN (1970s)

- In Canada for treatment for his ear trouble, Lilian's husband Lester Nicholson ('Nick') fell down a flight of hospital stairs and died.
- Dan's shoulder was injured yet again when one of the cross beams in the church bell tower fell on him.
- Brigadier Winstanley died in an accident on the hunting field.
- In 1972, Jack Woolley tripped in a rabbit hole and sprained his ankle.
- A year later he was clubbed down by burglars at Grey Gables and didn't recover consciousness for several days. Three months later he suffered a heart attack when his wife Valerie demanded a divorce.
- In the same year, 6-year-old Elizabeth was rushed to hospital after eating grain that had been treated with mercury.
- Laura cracked her teeth when the post bus was hijacked by robbers.
- Jethro Larkin broke his leg falling through the hayloft floor at Brookfield.
- Market-garden worker Arthur Tovey died when his ladder touched an overhead power cable.
- George Barford's son Terry attacked Joe Grundy whom he wrongly thought was poaching. Terry then crashed his car into a lamp post.
- Brian, newly married to Jennifer, wondered what he'd taken

on when Debbie cut herself on a milk bottle and had to have stitches, closely followed by Adam being bitten by an adder. Adam was saved by a miracle new serum, just available.

- Laura Archer burnt her arm in a chip pan fire.
- Christine's husband Paul Johnson was killed in a car crash in Germany.

A CHRISTMAS COMPLAINT

Lizzie Larkin and Nora Salt sang a duet called
'The Housewives' Lament' at the Christmas Revue in 1976.

MEMBERS OF HASSETT HILLS MARKETING GROUP

Hassett Hills lamb is a prime lamb brand established by a group of Borsetshire farmers to add value to their meat. Members of the marketing group include:

Adam Macy   Nick Spring   Sean
Ruth and David Archer Bill Oldfield   Terry Hodges

LIFE SWAP

In 2005, Ambridge embarked on a life/wife swap experiment to raise money for the fighting fund for the hoped-for restoration of The Cat and Fiddle. With interesting consequences…

SWAP 1:
SID AND JOLENE WITH OLIVER AND CAROLINE

Sid squirmed as the pub's part-owner Caroline queried his efficiency measures and asked about margins; Oliver squirmed when Jolene alluringly painted her toenails in front of a *Prisoner: Cell Block H* DVD.

SWAP 2:
DAVID AND RUTH WITH ROBERT AND LYNDA

Following the draw, David feared the worst but apart from Lynda turning Jill's prospective Flower and Produce Show marrow into Courgettes Provençales for supper, he and Lynda spent an unexpectedly enjoyable evening playing Cluedo with the children, while Ruth was pampered by Robert at Ambridge Hall.

SWAP 3:
EDDIE AND CLARRIE WITH
(1) BERT AND FREDA
(2) MATT AND LILIAN

Eddie had looked forward to dining like a king on Freda's cooking, but when she and Bert had to drop out, a new swap was hastily arranged with Matt and Lilian. It all worked out for the best: quailing at the ready-skinned rabbit Clarrie had intended for supper, Lilian treated the Grundy men to a slap-up dinner out, while Clarrie frolicked in the hot tub and won £50 when Matt took her to the races.

SWAP 4:
RICHARD AND SABRINA THWAITE WITH MARCUS
AND MADELEINE HENDRICKS

The first time anyone in Ambridge really got to know much about WAG-wannabe Sabrina and her mild-mannered husband Richard was when, as a result of the swap, she shacked up briefly with Marcus Hendricks, returning to Richard a few days later. She has since become a fixture in village life.

AN ACCIDENT
WAITING TO HAPPEN (1980s)

* Shula's new boyfriend, Mark Hebden, was kicked in the head by a deer he was trying to rescue from a lurcher.
* Lizzie Larkin died suddenly in 1980 and her husband Jethro in a farm accident in 1987.
* Polly Perks was killed and Pat was badly shaken when a milk tanker skidded into Polly's car in February 1982.
* 3-year-old William Grundy nearly choked on a sweet.
* Brian was kicked in the head by a BSE-infected cow at Grange Farm, causing a blood clot on the brain and a cerebral abscess. He later suffered from post-traumatic epilepsy, now thankfully abated.
* David suffered a black eye when Jethro hit him accidentally with a shovel; he then needed stitches when he cut his hand on a chainsaw.
* Pat broke a rib when she was kicked by a cow.

ESSENTIAL FACTS: LOWER LOXLEY

1. Elizabeth is not a big film buff; she'd rather curl up with a good book.
2. Lower Loxley gardener Titcombe is 'not the most articulate man in the world'.
3. Julia Pargetter's unpublished book is in a bottom drawer at Lower Loxley, waiting to be discovered.
4. Bert works as a guide at Lower Loxley.
5. At Lower Loxley, visitors end their tour of the house by going down the back stairs and coming out through the old servants' entrance. Straight

ahead is the old stable block with the shop and the Orangery café.

6. Nigel no longer has a car and rides his pushbike whenever possible.

7. The memorial at Lower Loxley to Rupert Pargetter is designed as a place of contemplation.

8. In 2003, Nigel made two greenwood stools, one for each of the twins.

9. Nigel's sister Camilla is married to James and has a son, Piers.

10. Toby works with the heavy horses and Jessica is the falconer.

EDDIE GRUNDY'S GNOMES

Eddie started making garden ornaments in 2001 in a bid to boost the Grundys' income. Early attempts at stone animals and classical statues were soon joined by a range of decorative gnomes. Favourite designs include:

- Fisherman gnome – holds a fishing rod. The classic, popular with gnome aficionados such as Derek Fletcher and Mr Pullen, who has a garden full of Eddie's ornaments. Sadly the example which Lilian gifted to Home Farm was clipped by the lawnmower and fell apart (or so Jennifer claimed).

- Butcher gnome – sports an apron and cleaver. This was the design for 'Lucky', the gnome which brought good fortune to Bert in a *Borchester Echo* competition and subsequently to the Ambridge cricket team, until he was stolen from outside The Bull by their Darrington rivals, and a stark threat received: 'Drop Adam Macy, or the gnome gets it!'

- Santa gnome – in festive gear. Specially created for the

'Grundy World of Christmas', this basically involved a swift repaint of some standard gnomes.

- 🦋 Mooning gnome – best not described. Created to Clarrie's horror.
- 🦋 Wolf-whistling gnome – Having sold only two Venus de Milos and a squirrel at a car boot, Eddie concluded he needed a unique selling point for his ornaments and came up with the idea of a movement-triggered wolf-whistling gnome. Predictably, this led to complaints to the Parish Council about noise pollution in Ambridge but Sundial House, the centre for disabled children, were delighted to take two for their sensory garden.

JILL ARCHER'S FRIENDS

Jill may not have family of her own (an orphan, she was living with an aunt at Crudley when Phil met her in 1957 and drew her into the bosom of the Archers) but she has the gift of friendship – and not just within the village.

SCHOOL PAL

An old school friend in London came to the rescue when, following Elizabeth's operation to correct her heart condition in 1972, Jill was emotionally and physically exhausted. She departed for a brief break and returned three months later, thankfully restored to loving wife and mother.

FRENCH LEAVE

Jill met Sheila Ferguson at a French class at Borchester Tech in 1977. Her new friend promptly suggested a short break in Paris, though Phil might well have borrowed the torch song of Sheila's Three Degrees namesake and asked 'When Will I See You Again?'

as their three days away turned into ten. Nor was he reassured when Andre, Gaston and Maurice as well as the more prosaic Henry and Clive – from Scarborough of all places – featured in Jill's holiday reminiscences, though she assured him it was all '*tout innocent*'.

THE MERRY WIDOW

Phil and Jill met lively widow Diana in America on their round-the-world trip to celebrate their Golden Wedding. Diana was soon offering Jill another break from Ambridge routine – in Sidmouth, where she lived. But though Jill loved the unspoilt town of Sidmouth itself, and its many picturesque attractions, just as with her French leave thirty years before, she was relieved to get home after a whirlwind week.

ILLNESSES AND AILMENTS (1980s)

- ❧ Tony got tetanus and was rushed to Intensive Care.
- ❧ Jennifer got orf (a skin irritation) from one of the sheep.
- ❧ Shula suffered from endometriosis.
- ❧ Laura Archer slipped in the woods and broke her ankle. She was taken to hospital and discharged but died of heart failure six days later.
- ❧ Emma Carter went through a phase of bed-wetting. It returned in 1994 when her mother was in prison.
- ❧ Kenton returned to Borsetshire with a thyroid deficiency.
- ❧ Newly arrived townie Lynda Snell turned out to suffer badly from hay fever.
- ❧ Following his head injury, Brian suffered post-traumatic epilepsy.
- ❧ Emma Carter was born with jaundice in 1984 and Christopher four years later with a cleft lip and palate.
- ❧ Nigel's father, Gerald, died of cancer.

SOME SHARED MEMORIES

Dan and Doris's elder son, Jack, was born a year to the day after their wedding – 17 December 1921 and 17 December 1922.

Debbie's birthday (24 December 1970) is the same day as Shula and Alistair's wedding anniversary nearly thirty years later (24 December 1999).

Daniel Hebden Lloyd and Ruairi Donovan share a birthday – 14 November – though they were born twelve years apart, in 1994 and 2002 respectively.

Joe Grundy and David Archer also share a birthday – 18 September 1921 and 18 September 1958.

So do Eddie Grundy and Ben Archer – 15 March 1951 and 15 March 2002.

Lilian's first marriage and Jennifer's second both occurred on the same date – 26 May, though seven years apart – 1969 and 1976.

Obviously not superstitious, or more likely ignorant of the connection, Caroline and Oliver Sterling were married on 29 June 2006, the same date as the ill-fated and short-lived marriage of John Tregorran to Janet Sheldon in 1963.

Kate Aldridge and Lucas Madikane were married on 12 April 2001, principally so that Kate could gain residency in South Africa. William and Emma Grundy were divorced on 12 April 2006.

SOME NEAR MISSES

Abbie Tucker (Abigail Elizabeth to give her her full name) almost shares a birthday with Peggy's late mother, Mrs P: Abbie was born on 7 March 2008, Mrs P on 6 March 1905.

Jennifer's two daughters by Brian were born almost exactly eleven years apart – Kate on 30 September 1977 and Alice on 29 September 1988. Alice's birthday is also the same day as the date of Nigel and Elizabeth's wedding in 1994.

Tom and Pru Forrest, Ambridge's most devoted couple, died just six days apart – Tom on 5 November and Pru on 11 November 1998.

MISCELLANEOUS AMBRIDGE RESIDENTS OF THE 1970s AND THEIR DESCRIPTIONS

Mrs Pearson	Old Age Pensioner
Mrs Jessop	Over-60s member
Mrs Galloway	Speaker for the W.I.
Mr Benson	Another OAP
Mrs Chadwick	Has a daughter

AN ACCIDENT WAITING TO HAPPEN (1990s)

- Mike Tucker lost his sight in one eye after an accident on the Estate.
- Mandy Beesborough sprained her wrist in a riding accident at Home Farm, to Brian's consternation.
- Days later Alice fell off a gate and gashed her forehead, also to Brian's consternation.
- In a horrific precursor of the accident which was to kill him, a tractor with a faulty handbrake rolled back into John Archer in 1992, injuring his leg.
- 1995 was a bad year for the Frys: Bert caught his hand badly on a nail and Freda dropped a catering-size frozen lasagne on her foot.
- 14-year-old William was knocked off his bike by a lorry working for the Estate. The Grundys claimed compensation.

- Phil cracked a rib when he lost his footing getting down from a tractor.
- Shula's husband, Mark, died in a car crash which also injured Caroline.
- When she was four, David almost ran Pip over in the Brookfield yard. Three years later, she slipped into the bull pen to retrieve her ball and he had to act quickly to scoop her out.
- John Archer died in a tractor accident.
- A month later, Tom broke his toe.
- Roy was beaten up by racists who'd previously thrown acid into Usha Gupta's face.
- Jill suffered a transverse fracture of the patella when she slipped on a toy car left on the stairs by one of the children.

PARISH COUNCIL

Chair: Derek Fletcher
Vice Chair: Vacancy
Clerk to the Council: Christine Barford
Committee: David Archer, Neil Carter, Lynda Snell, Lilian Bellamy

AMBRIDGE OPERETTA

In 1977, the Queen's Silver Jubilee year, the Ambridge Chorale was under the joint tutelage of Phil Archer and, channelling his Welsh roots, Pat's uncle, Haydn Evans. Haydn came up with the idea of a Gilbert and Sullivan concert which pulled in such diverse participants as gamekeeper and local lothario Gordon Armstrong, better known for his judo skills, and Martha Woodford's husband, Joby, who must have learnt his words by rote as he was later discovered to be unable to read. The modest George Barford, originally charged with building the scenery, was eventually persuaded to sing: his solo from 'Ruddigore' turned out to be one of the evening's highlights.

SIX SHORTEST MARRIAGES
❧

Lilian and Lester Nicholson, known as Nick, were married after a whirlwind romance on 26 May 1969, but Canadian Nick died in his home country on 18 March 1970.

After years of thinking she would never meet Mr Right, Caroline married Guy Pemberton on 11 September 1995. Sadly Mr Right was Mr Not In The Best Of Health: Guy died on 12 April 1996.

William and Emma Grundy's doomed marriage limped along from 27 August 2004 to 29 September 2005, when Emma told her devastated husband she had to follow her heart and was leaving him for his brother Edward.

Though everyone thought that he and Carol Grey, later Grenville, were the ideal couple, long-time bachelor John Tregorran settled on Janet Sheldon, Ambridge's district nurse. But they were married only briefly – just four months after walking down the aisle on 29 June 1963, she died in a car crash on 31 October.

Phil Archer and Grace Fairbrother, after an agonising four-year, on-off-on-again courtship, managed only five months of marriage. They became man and wife on Easter Monday, 11 April, 1955, but Grace died following a fire at the stables on 22 September the same year.

Julia Pargetter also enjoyed just over five months of late-flowering love with husband Lewis Carmichael: they married on 26 May 2005; Julia died on 7 November the same year.

ESSENTIAL FACTS:
CAROLINE AND OLIVER

1. When Caroline first arrived in Ambridge, she worked at The Bull. She has previously run a wine bar in Bristol.
2. Oliver's ex-wife is called Jane. They divorced amicably once their children had grown up.
3. Oliver is no good at plastering.
4. When Caroline was selling The Dower House, she caught Matt and Lilian, who were viewing it, trying out the bed.
5. One of Oliver's daughters lives in America with her husband. They visited Europe in the summer of 2009 and Oliver and Caroline met up with them for a few days in France.
6. Caroline has brown eyes.
7. She can play golf.
8. Oliver was self-conscious about losing his hair until Caroline explained that a good haircut was the secret. She took him to her hairdresser, Kim.
9. Caroline has a godmother called Louise who has good taste.
10. Caroline and Oliver used to be foster parents.

ENTER
WALTER GABRIEL

'Hello, me old pal, me old beauty!' From the 1950s to the late 1980s, this greeting, delivered with a throaty chuckle, heralded the arrival of Dan's old friend Walter, a disreputable farmer and all-out village 'character'. In the 1951 election, Walter declared he would vote for anyone who promised him £10 a week for life and free beer. His often-quoted granny had 16 children and 48 grandchildren, but the apple of Walter's eye was his only son, 'my Nelson'. In 1967, Nelson was famously accused of the Borchester Mail Van Robbery. He faked his own disappearance, was finally caught by Interpol, tried... and acquitted.

THE RECTOR'S WIFE

Richard Adamson was vicar of Ambridge from 1973 to 1988, but the family found it hard to manage on his stipend. His wife Dorothy took on a variety of jobs:

CURRICULUM VITAE

Name	DOROTHY ADAMSON (MRS)
Address	The Vicarage, Ambridge, Borsetshire
Date of Birth	14.01.1945

EMPLOYMENT HISTORY

October 1975–January 1976

Manor Court, Ambridge
Assistant at Market Garden (part-time)

Duties:	Weighing produce from Pick Your Own, dealing with customers, Cutting and packing salads and vegetables.
Reason for leaving:	Seasonal work
Referee:	Mrs Carol Tregorran, Manor Court, Ambridge

January–April 1976

Gear Change Boutique, West St, Borchester
Sales Assostant

Duties:	Assisting customers, pricing and arranging stock, operation of till.
Reason for leaving:	Business closed
Referee:	Mr Otto Gibson, 9 West St, Borchester.

June–September 1976

Further study:
Course to be Playgroup Leader whilst helping at Playgroup.

<u>October 1976–October 1979</u>

Playgroup leader (voluntary)

<u>October 1979–May 1987</u>

Village Shop and Post Office, Ambridge
Sales assistant

Duties: Dealing with customers,
                      handling money, using till,
                      pricing and arranging stock
Reason for leaving: Seeking new opportunity
Referee: Mr Jack Woolley, Grey Gables Country House
                      Hotel, Ambridge

<u>July 1987–May 1988</u>

Ambridge Surgery, Ambridge
Receptionist

Duties: Dealing with patients,
                      booking appointments,
                      giving test results,
                      maintaining patient records
Reason for leaving: Husband relocated to North East
Referee: Dr Matthew Thorogood,
                      Ambridge Surgery, Ambridge

<u>INTERESTS</u>

Parish activities eg Playgroup, Mother's Union, fete committee
Cookery
Gardening
Making corn dollies
Helper at Riding for Disabled

AMBRIDGE TALENT

Alice	was in the school choir
Bert	can versify, do monologues, adapt pantomimes, act and direct
Brenda	can sing and dance
Brian	played the guitar as a student
Christine	like her mother Doris, has a good voice
Debbie	learnt the piano as a child
Elizabeth	was a good piano player as a child
Emma	can dance
Ed	can sing and play the guitar
Eddie	can sing and play the guitar but is no good at telling jokes
Fallon	can sing, play the guitar and compose
Hayley	can sing, write poetry, adapt pantomimes and do stand-up
Joe	can act, tell tales, recite long poems and do monologues
Jolene	can sing, dance, play the guitar and keyboards
Kenton	thinks he is a comedian
Lynda	can't act, sing or dance but she can direct
Neil	can sometimes be persuaded to tell jokes
Phil	plays the piano and the organ
Robert	can't sing but has tried to play the guitar
Roy	wrote a poem for his friend John's funeral
Shula	used to play the guitar and sing
Tom	can sing

IN THE PAST

- Dan and Doris were known for their duets.
- Dan said Walter's voice was 'like a rusty nail being driven through the bottom of a cocoa tin'.

- George Barford played the cornet in the Hollerton Silver Band.
- Phil used to help run the Ambridge Chorale.
- Eddie released a record – A-side 'Lambs to the Slaughter' and B-side 'Clarrie's Song'.

ILLNESSES AND AILMENTS (1990s)

- Phil needed a hip replacement.
- Shula had a failed attempt at IVF.
- After fearing that her young son Daniel had leukaemia, it was almost a relief to Shula when, instead, Systemic Juvenile Rheumatoid Arthritis was diagnosed in 1998.
- Pru Forrest suffered a stroke which robbed her of her speech.
- Marjorie Antrobus had a cataract operation. A second followed in 2000.
- Mike Tucker suffered from depression, as did Pat after the death of John.
- Julia Pargetter's alcoholism was treated in a drying-out clinic.

BY GEORGE!

A wall safe in the old Ambridge vicarage was found to
contain Parish Records going back to 1706.

COMPASSIONATE CLARRIE

It should really be Clarrie, not Joe, who bears a grudge against the Archer family. Not once but twice (the second time fatally) her dear dad Jethro suffered in farm accidents at Brookfield. In July 1975, he fell through the floor of the hayloft. He was prodded into claiming compensation by union man Mike Tucker and received his cheque the following October. In June 1987, he was less lucky when, lopping a tree with David, he was crushed by a falling branch and died from internal bleeding. At the funeral a magnanimous Clarrie told a remorseful David that she didn't hold him responsible.

A ROYAL PROPOSAL

David proposed to Sophie Barlow whilst watching
the Royal Wedding of Prince Andrew and Sarah Ferguson.

AN ACCIDENT
WAITING TO HAPPEN (2000s)

- David started the new Millennium with injuries sustained rescuing a cow which had slipped down a bank into the Am and which trampled him in its panic.
- Debbie jumped from a hay bale only to land on a piece of wood with a nail sticking out. It pierced her foot.
- Emma was badly injured when Ed crashed a car he'd been driving illegally. She suffering permanent scarring to her leg.
- Ed was later beaten up when he tried to stop Emma's mobile being stolen after a night out.
- George Barford was beaten up by a vengeful Clive Horrobin.
- Jazzer ended up in a drug-induced coma.
- Nigel broke his left collarbone in a quad bike race with Kenton.
- David hurt his shoulder practising for a fundraising soap box derby on Lakey Hill.

- A cow kicked David above the eyebrow, requiring hospital attention and stitches.
- Ed Grundy broke his toe when he slipped off a rock at the seaside; a couple of months later, his brother William nearly strangled him in a fist-fight.
- Freddie Pargetter hurt his leg when he fell down the Lower Loxley ha-ha.
- David knocked Alan Franks off his motorbike just two days before his wedding, leaving him with a limp for the ceremony.
- Caroline broke her upper arm in an accident at the Lower Loxley Team Chase.

WISE WORDS FROM MRS P

One of Mrs P's favourite sayings was:
'There's a price to be paid for everything in this life.
Especially if it shaves.'

EIGHT SPECTACULAR STORIES

- Tony's misplaced glasses lay at the bottom of the wet grain pit for a year, having fallen out of his pocket when it was being cleaned out. They weren't discovered until the job was tackled again the following summer. Initially too mean to buy a new pair, he wore his old ones, held together with tape, until Pat managed to stand on them. He was then talked into a 'designer' pair, to Pat's relief.
- Brian hates to admit he needs glasses but once had to get Matt to read the small print on a fertiliser bag.

- Alan's ex-mother-in-law Mabel Thompson wears glasses and often mislays them.

- When Ed and Emma were considering running away to France, the couple who were interested in taking Ed on made their living as a writer (her) and seller of sunglasses over the internet (him).

- Lynda wore sunglasses when meeting the private detective she'd engaged to follow Robert, thinking he was having an affair. In fact, he was about to go bankrupt.

- When Jill first had to have reading glasses in 1978, she found it demoralising.

- Following Mike's farm accident and detached retina in 1991, he wore dark glasses for many months.

- Worryingly, Walter didn't have his eyes tested until 1960, by which time he was already driving the school bus. After an eye test in 1968 found that his vision was declining, he gave up driving altogether.

SOME ESSENTIAL FACTS

1. Freda wears support stockings for work.
2. Lilian has a state-of-the-art juicing machine.
3. In the garden at Home Farm there is a pergola with a white rose that blooms in June.
4. Sid is very competitive.
5. The Wimberton cricket team are known as The Wimbles because they play on a common.
6. Matt and Lilian enjoy and are good at ballroom dancing.
7. In her youth, Pat was county champion at javelin.
8. Fallon did GCSE Spanish.
9. Red wine gives Bert heartburn.
10. Mr Pullen has a home help.

ILLNESSES AND AILMENTS (2000s)

- Brian, Christine and Tony suffered intermittently with bad backs.
- Helen Archer suffered an eating disorder.
- Jack Woolley was diagnosed with Alzheimer's Disease.
- Bert insisted on working even though he had terrible flu. David had to send him home and insist on semi-retirement.
- Lynda infected the entire cast of the 2008 pantomime with flu.
- Peggy Woolley had a stroke which left her with impaired vision on one side.
- Having foolishly put off the heart operation recommended after the birth of the twins, Elizabeth collapsed in the Orangery café. The cardiac catheterisation eventually performed was a success.
- Ruth was diagnosed with breast cancer and had a mastectomy, followed a few years later by a breast reconstruction.
- Julia Pargetter and Betty Tucker died within six weeks of each other, of a stroke and a heart attack respectively.
- Matt feigned frequent illness, unable to face up to his financial and fraud problems.

SHEEP NUTS

David and Ruth's three-month-old marriage hit a rocky patch in early 1989 when she ticked him off, telling him that the cut-price sheep nuts he'd bought could be responsible for an outbreak of twin-lamb disease in the flock.

TONY DOWN UNDER

Amazingly, years before Kenton made a life there, Tony considered emigrating to Australia. As an 18-year-old in 1969, he was so restless it seemed that even the gift of a fishing rod from Uncle Tom and the purchase of a scooter wouldn't be enough to keep him in the village. Ralph Bellamy, his then boss, had the answer. A research trip to Cambridgeshire to study sprout-growing left Tony proselytising for change: this was the way forward! The arrival in Ambridge of a drill capable of sowing 12 acres of sprouts a day on Bellamy's land sealed his fate. Tony stayed.

VILLAGE WEBSITE COMMITTEE MEMBERS AND RESPONSIBILITIES

Jennifer	Chair; Village History and the Village Year
Usha	Treasurer
Jolene	Leisure News
Lynda	Church/Parish News
Joe	Country Notes

CALENDAR BOYS

When a fund-raising idea for the Borsetshire Rural Stress Line was needed, a male 'nude' calendar seemed the obvious idea. These were the Ambridge pin-ups:

Mr January	Mike Tucker with pintas
Mr February	Jean-Paul with a French loaf
Mr March	Eddie Grundy with strategically placed oilcan
Mr April	Bert Fry
Mr May	Roy Tucker
Mr June	Sid Perks
Mr July	Greg Turner
Mr August	William Grundy
Mr September	Simon Gerrard
Mr October	Owen King (aka Gareth Taylor)
Mr November	Dr Tim Hathaway with stethoscope
Mr December	All eleven on Heydon Berrow wearing Santa hats, beards, and clutching strategically placed holly

DICING WITH DEATH

Carol Tregorran's market garden manager, Arthur Tovey, died in 1976 at the tragically young age of 41 when an aluminium ladder he was carrying touched an overhead power cable. In his brief time in Ambridge, he seems to have both courted and attracted danger. Arriving in the village as a 35-year old bachelor, he announced that his hobby was stock-car racing and then promptly got himself trapped in an apple store whose contents were giving off a noxious gas. Maybe he knew he wasn't long for this world, for he'd had the foresight to make a will in which he instructed Carol's husband John to distribute his £9,000 savings to charity. The inquest recorded a verdict of death by misadventure.

AN AFRICAN ADVENTURE

Christine rarely leaves the village these days, and then only to go and stay with her adopted son Peter in London, but once her horizons were – or could have been – much wider. In the 1950s she had not one but two chances to go to Africa. The first came through a chance encounter with the eccentric Lady Hylberow, but her Ladyship cooled on the idea of Christine accompanying her to view pre-Coptic churches in Ethiopia when she discovered that Christine 'ran around with young men' and wrote to Doris accordingly. Two years later a proposal from the Squire's nephew, no less, could have taken Christine to Kenya, where he'd inherited a farm. But she turned him down.

LADY HYLBEROW'S LETTER TO DORIS

Dear Mrs Archer

After very careful thought, I have decided to write to you rather than to Christine to advise you that I have decided against taking her with me to Ethiopia. I have no doubt this decision will bring considerable relief to you and your husband, though a certain amount of disappointment to Christine.

Recent events have led me to change my opinions somewhat with regard to your daughter, whom I at first imagined to be an ideal type of girl, refined and ladylike in every way. I now find that, in common with many other youngsters of this day and age, she possesses a shallower nature than I had thought and her main interest would seem to be concerned with 'boy-friends' as she calls them. In view of this I would prefer not to have the responsibility of looking after her in circumstances where she might have opportunities for furthering these regrettable interests to a possibly alarming extent. For example, aboard ship and in France and Italy, the Latin races being of a notoriously 'romantic' disposition.

Perhaps you will tell Christine of my decision as kindly as possible. I am yours….

OLD SEA DOG

After buying one of the Brookfield barn conversions in the late 1980s, Godfrey Wendover courted Peggy before she rekindled her romance with Jack Woolley. A widower who'd done well in insurance after leaving the Navy, he'd retained many naval habits, such as a fondness for pink gin and, indeed, a beard. (Tony called him 'Captain Pugwash'.) If he did go on a bit, at least some of his yarns were amusing, such as his recollections of Officer Training during the war, when torpedo training was based at the commandeered Roedean school. The dormitories had bell pushes with the advice: 'If you need a mistress, press the bell.' Peggy's reaction to this anecdote is not recorded.

BACK TO SCHOOL

AMBRIDGE CHILDREN AND THEIR SCHOOLS (SEPTEMBER 2009)

Ruairi Donovan	Loxley Barrett Infant and Junior
Ben Archer	Loxley Barrett Infant and Junior
Lily and Freddie Pargetter	Loxley Barrett Infant and Junior
George Grundy	Loxley Barrett Infant and Junior
Jake Hanson	Loxley Barrett Infant and Junior
Phoebe Tucker	Borchester Green
Josh Archer	Borchester Green
Jamie Perks	Borchester Green
Daniel Hebden Lloyd	Felpersham Cathedral School
Pip Archer	6th form at Borchester College – AS/A levels and GCSE Agricultural Sciences

There are school buses to Loxley Barrett and Borchester Green which pick up and drop off outside The Bull. Shula is in a lift-share to Felpersham.

SOME MORE
ESSENTIAL FACTS

1. Tom says that village quiz team supremo Nathan Booth's idea of a good night in is a glass of lemonade and a couple of hours with his Rubik's cube.

2. Jack's carer, Barney, has had to leave to take care of his own father.

3. Rapist Gareth Taylor's other two names were Owen King and Marcus Dixon.

4. Bert started 'walking out' with Freda after winning a ploughing match.

5. Phoebe is friends with Molly Button: they go to play at each other's houses.

6. Tom loves tapas.

7. There is a conservatory at the Lodge, as well as a summerhouse, a sundial and a bird table.

8. The Cat and Fiddle has been converted into flats and there are people living there.

9. Moles Croft Farm in Loxley Norton is the site of the anaerobic digester.

10. Lilian has no interest in sport.

A FARMER'S JOURNAL

Dan's 1950s farm account books-cum-diary make interesting reading.
A scrupulous record-keeper, he noted:

1951

January   Herd (Dairy Shorthorn) entered as Attested. Gain of extra
4d per gallon on milk price.

Phil nagging me to replace Blossom and Boxer with
tractor.

February   Walter says he will buy Boxer. Blossom to be put out to grass.

April   Sowing schedule a month behind owing to bad weather.
Ground not dry enough to get wheat in.

July   Cow gained 4th place at Borchester Show: 'Very Highly
Commended'. Doris chuffed!

September   3 down-calvers sold @ £129 each.

1 Shorthorn bought @ 82 guineas (yield 1200 gallons per
annum).

Sheep not fat enough for sale this year: will run on till
next year.

October   Daisy calves down. Six more due before end of month.

Get Bill to prepare field next to Five Acre for winter
wheat.

Complaint from factory about dirt tare on sugar beet. Crop
was 40 tons to the acre but they say not properly topped.
Speak Bill.

November Letter from Dairy re lowered butter-fat content. Mystery.

Could be beet tops in feed – too much carbohydrate?

❧ 1952 ❧

January	Six low-fat content cows identified: to be sold. New egg-washer arrives.
February	Low fat-content cows replaced with 2 high-quality Shorthorns @100 guineas Herd size now 14; average value £50 each.
March	To Craven Arms sheep sales: bought 40 nice-looking Clun ewes, in lamb; £8/11/- apiece.
May	Binder playing up. To speed haymaking, intend using contractor with elevator to help bring in.
June	1st - Blossom foaled – a big colt. Hay all in. Good crop – but will feel the real benefit after Christmas!
July	Twenty-seven days without rain. Winter wheat in Five Acre never looked better.
August	Plane crashes on Five Acre!
September	15 sheep ready for market. Will buy replacements as plenty beet tops for winter feed. Second Prize Borchester Show for Amber – Best of Breeds. Doris very chuffed.
October	Going to try Nord Duprez variety winter wheat – 42/- per cwt.
November	Jack has covered stack of beet with straw to keep off the frost.
December	Imperial Hotel, Borchester, to take all the turkeys this year.

Reggie Trentham may have found horse for Christine. Name: Midnight.

❧ 1953 ❧

January   District Officer advises treatment of sugar beet land before ploughing as crop deprives the soil of phosphates.

February District Officer thinks Brookfield land may be suited for lucerne (called alfalfa in some countries). Not sure. Does not attain full development for 2 or 3 seasons.

March   District Officer here to take soil samples in possible field for lucerne. Soil must contain sufficient lime to render crop alkaline. Advises I feed soil with potash, lime and phosphate. Expense??
    Simon has built lambing pen in orchard.
    Must get Blossom's foal used to halter for handling.

May   Crystal and Clara averaging only 50 gallons per month. Sold @ £53 and £48 apiece.
    Looks like swine fever at piggery.

June   Replacement cow bought, Hollerton Market, from Mr Weatherby. £75.

July   Achieved good price for young lambs at market.

November Hammer Mill and feed mixer installed. Looks good!
    Pullets transferred from free range to deep litter. New method – worth a try.

❧ 1954 ❧

January   Bitter weather.

April   After cold winter, little sign of spring.

May   Squire called re: selling up in Ambridge. Said it had been a hard decision. Given us first refusal on Brookfield. Didn't sleep for worrying.

      Been to see bank manager. Reckon I can raise money to buy. Doris very excited.

June   More rain. Haymaking delayed yet again.

August   More rain. Now corn harvest delayed.

September   Yields above average despite weather. Small mercies, especially as am to be owner of Brookfield Farm!

❧ 1955 ❧

January   Intend trying new Friesian breed. Also – with regret – to sell Blossom.

      Terrible flooding. Appeals for help to distressed farmers on wireless. Can spare half a ton of hay.

February   New Friesian cow bought: gave 3 ½ gallons! Excellent!

      Refused offer of £35 for Blossom's foal – dealer turned out to be a knacker. Told him no deal.

March   Average 1 ¾ lambs per ewe this lambing. Blossom sold.

April   12th Got sugar beet in today as ground in good tilth.

May   Going to try an early hay crop ('silage') from Amos Atkins' place.

June   Haymaking – all hands to the fork! Simon, Len, Walter, Jack, John T., even P.C. Bryden lent a hand.

July   5th Len hoeing beet.

October   Wheat and barley yields excellent. Sugar beet down – this
            season too dry for it. Who'd be a farmer?

Sadly, just three months later, Dan lost his entire dairy herd – by now up
to 18 cows and 30 followers – when they had to be slaughtered following
an outbreak of foot-and-mouth, as did his entire flock of sheep (40 ewes
and 30 lambs), as well as 5 sows and 48 young pigs. Dan went through a
period of deep depression and though by October he'd rallied enough to
restock, buying seven cows, six newly calved heifers and eighty Radnor-
type sheep and two Downland rams, he never resumed his journals.

PAROCHIAL CHURCH COUNCIL

Chair: Alan Franks
Church Wardens: Neil Carter, Christine Barford
Committee: Bert Fry, Jill Archer, Susan Carter and Jean Harvey

Places

ST STEPHEN'S CHURCH

THE VICAR

Alan Franks, who came to the church in his forties after training as an accountant, has been Ambridge's vicar since 2003. After the death of his first wife Catherine, who was Jamaican, Alan brought up their daughter Amy with help (and some homilies/home truths) from his Bradford-based mother-in-law Mabel Thompson. Alan caused something of a stir amongst his congregation, notably Shula, when he announced his engagement to local solicitor Usha Gupta. Their respective families took some persuading, too, but had accepted, if not wholly endorsed, the match by the time Alan and Usha married in successive Hindu and Christian ceremonies in August 2008.

ALAN'S FOUR PARISHES

- Ambridge
- Penny Hassett
- Edgeley
- Darrington

He may also be required to help out in

- Netherbourne
- Loxley Barrett
- Lakey Green

WINSTON'S MOUND

There is a small cairn in the garden of Honeysuckle Cottage. It marks the grave of Nelson's daughter Rosemary's dog, Winston.

VIVA ESPANA

In 1964, John Tregorran took himself off to Spain for six months to get over the death of his wife Janet in a car crash. On his return he set up a small Spanish-style *bodega* at Grey Gables for Jack Woolley, presumably to cash in on the number of people beginning to take package holidays to the Costas.

COPPER-BOTTOMED

While Dan and Doris holidayed in Ireland with fellow farming friends Fred and Betty Barratt, thieves broke into Brookfield and stole Doris's prized collection of copper, including, ironically, a copper sailing ship which had been a present from Betty following a previous holiday to Guernsey. As a new arrival in the village, one of the chief suspects was Roger Patillo, also known as Roger Travers-Macy, and soon to become Jennifer's husband. Though the burglars also took some silverware, somewhat insultingly, Doris's jewellery was left untouched. She must have had her best pieces with her.

GRANGE SPINNEY

This small development of executive homes (and four starter homes) between the churchyard and Grange Farm has become the Wisteria Lane of Ambridge. Residents include:

- Sabrina Thwaite and her 'tanorexic' friends Minette, Abi and Karen – the 'Bling-a-Roses'. Sabrina drives her two young daughters to school each day in a vast 4x4. She and her husband Richard have added a large conservatory which is almost as big as the house. David blushes when Sabrina's name is mentioned.

- Mrs Noakes, who has also started to cause David trouble, complaining to him in his capacity as Parish Councillor about mud on the roads and the destruction of her staddle stone by a careless driver (Will Grundy, in fact). She also complains about bell-ringing practice. Reportedly built like a tank, she has dark hair with badger stripes and a big nose. Her daughter Harriet has a horse in livery at The Stables but is hardly ever around to ride it as she goes to boarding school. Both Noakes parents work in Felpersham and shop there in preference to the village shop. They play golf.

- Barry Simmonds, who is single, and with good reason: his hair looks as if it's been cut with a tin-opener, he stuffs crisp packets under the cushions at The Bull, and he has slug-like lips. Unfortunately for Kirsty, he has a serious crush on her and once tried to impress her by cartwheeling across the pub garden.

- Mrs Palmer, who wears a lot of jewellery and was heard to wonder if Alan and Usha were getting married in a mosque.

- Madeleine and Marcus Hendricks, who famously 'life-swapped' with the Thwaites.

- The Robinsons, who have a dog, and the nondescript McWilliamses and Thompsons.

THE RETURN OF JOLENE

Clarrie's hair may well have stood on end when, in 1996, she ran into Jolene Rogers, the so-called 'Lily of Layton Cross' at the hairdressers. Her old nemesis and rival for Eddie's affections had discarded her Dolly Parton wig and was having highlights put in her newly brunette hair. Jolene confided that she was back in Borsetshire after living in Huddersfield and had formed a new band, the Midnight Walkers. Soothed by Jolene's reassurances that there had never been anything between her and Eddie, big-hearted Clarrie even gave her blessing to a Jolene/Eddie duet of 'Phoenix from the Flames' at her birthday barbecue.

TRAINS

- ❧ Phil proposed to Jill at New Street Station, Birmingham (she was a travelling kitchen-appliance demonstrator at the time).
- ❧ Sid saw his daughter Lucy off to University from Hollerton Junction along with Betty Tucker (she was separated from Mike and Sid from Kathy at the time).
- ❧ One of the places Ed and Emma rejected as a place to live were the flats converted from the old engine shed at Hollerton Junction.
- ❧ Jill likes to be at the station/airport early enough to catch the train/plane before.
- ❧ Ambridge residents often enjoy a day out on the local steam railway, the Blackberry Line. Kate Aldridge's second daughter, Nolly, was nearly born on the train.

THE CHURCH CARPET

In 1995, Jill's B&B guests told her about the annual floral carpet in their church. Ambridge adopted the idea and bolted it onto that year's fete. The design was Saints and their Companion Animals, including St John's Eagle, a red cow for St Modwena, a pig for St Anthony of Egypt and a horse for St Stephen.

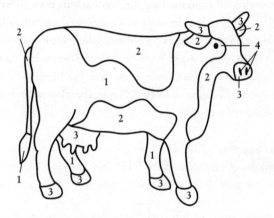

Flower Plan for St Modwena's Cow

Key:

1 Red Flowers
2 Orange Flowers
3 Pink Flowers
4 Purple Flowers

VILLAGE HALL COMMITTEE MEMBERS

Oliver Sterling / Jill Archer / Christine Barford

GREY GABLES

The four-star Grey Gables Country House Hotel is built in Victorian neo-Gothic style and nestles in 15 acres of gardens. There are 24 en-suite bedrooms in the main building and a further 36 in the annexe.

Facilities: bar, bistro, restaurant with dining terrace, excellent wine cellar, ballroom and function rooms.

The Health Club has an indoor pool, gym, jacuzzi, sauna and solarium.

The Health Food bar serves juices and light snacks.

DOCTOR ON CALL

With the departure of Tim Hathaway, Ambridge is now served by two different doctors' practices, one in Hollerton, six miles west, the other in Borchester, six miles north-east. The village is therefore divided:

PATIENTS AT THE BORCHESTER PRACTICE

Honeysuckle Cottage	Adam and Ian
1, The Green	Tom and Brenda
Willow Farm	Roy, Hayley, Phoebe and Abbie
Willow Cottage	Mike and Vicky
Ambridge View	Neil, Susan, Christopher
April Cottage	Kathy, Kenton, Jamie
Keeper's Cottage	Joe, Eddie, Clarrie
Casa Nueva	Will, Nic, Jake and Mia
Ambridge Hall	Lynda and Robert
Home Farm	Brian, Jennifer, Alice, Ruairi
The Stables	Shula, Alistair, Daniel
Brookfield	Ruth, David, Pip, Josh, Ben
The Bungalow	Bert and Freda

Rickyard Cottage	Emma, Ed and George
Bridge Farm	Pat and Tony

PATIENTS AT THE HOLLERTON PRACTICE

The Lodge	Peggy and Jack
The Bull	Sid, Jolene, Fallon
Woodbine Cottage	Christine
Glebe Cottage	Phil and Jill
The Vicarage	Alan and Usha
Grange Farm	Oliver and Caroline
The Dower House	Matt and Lilian

TEN FACTS ABOUT AMBRIDGE AND AROUND
❧

- In normal times you see a police car in Ambridge about once a month
- There are 'Please Drive Carefully' signs on approach roads to the village
- The Bengal Tiger will deliver to Ambridge
- There are Doggy bins
- The Ambridge Protection Society used to be headed by Laura Archer
- The first farm walk in Ambridge was at Brookfield in 1976
- The 'Nippy Chippy' van is in Ambridge on a Friday for fish and chips
- Nightingale Farm used to be an Arts Centre and Arkwright Hall a Youth Club
- The children's playground is actually D.A.M.P. – the Dan Archer Memorial Playground
- Matt Crawford made 'a small fortune' selling a wood he owned for the widening of the Borchester bypass

FIVE THINGS NOT TO MISS IN ST STEPHEN'S CHURCH

1. Lawson-Hope chapel
2. Alabaster tomb of Richard and Ann Lawson
3. The Woolhay monument
4. Grace Archer Memorial window
5. Plaque commemorating a peal rung in 1896 and reading:
    'The following members of Ambridge bell
    ringers rang a peal of 5,040 Grandsire Doubles
    on 1st October 1896: J. Archer, T. Forrest, F.
    Newcombe, S. Gabriel, A. Horrobin. The peal
    lasted three hours and twenty minutes.'

CARAVANNING DISASTERS

- When bearded University lecturer John Tregorran parked his green Romany caravan on Heydon Berrow in 1953, he was regarded with deep mistrust. Tom Forrest thought he recognised him as a poacher he'd stopped in the woods and Christine Archer suspected him of horse-rustling.
- After the failure of his pig-breeding scheme, Walter Gabriel had a caravan site.
- After their bankruptcy and the disaster of their council accommodation at the notorious Meadow Rise, the Grundys moved into a caravan back in Ambridge. Ed preferred the bender he built nearby.
- Neil bought a caravan as the Carters' temporary home while they (self)-built Ambridge View. Christopher rapidly deserted for the box room at Willow Farm and Emma moved into Will's flat at The Dower House.

218

The same caravan was later home to Ed, Emma and George but claustrophobia and the bitter winter cold contributed to their splitting up. Neil sold the ill-fated vehicle.

SOUTH BORSETSHIRE VILLAGES AND THEIR FACILITIES

PENNY HASSETT
Mission Hall
The Crown and Cushion – a posh pub
Sundial House – a centre for children with special needs

WATERLEY CROSS
Mont Blanc – a posh restaurant

LOXLEY BARRETT
Primary school
The Bear – pub
The Half Moon – gastro pub

LAYTON CROSS
There's a market held near Layton Cross at weekends

HOLLERTON
Hollerton Junction (station)
There is a garage on the Hollerton Road
There is a vets' practice in Hollerton
There's a pub in Hollerton called Gold,
but everyone calls it Stickies because of
all the beer that gets spilt on the dance floor
Branch library

DARRINGTON
Seafood restaurant
The Hare and Hounds – pub

HEYBURY
Has an annual fair
The Black Swan – pub
Heybury House hospice
Airfield (home to the Borchester Buzzards Hang Gliding Club)

BRAMPTON GREEN
Craft Centre

SWINGING SIXTIES

At the Grand Opening of the Cellar Club for the village's young people in 1963, the popular Borchester combo The Swingalongs were the main attraction – so much so that, by popular demand, they were back again the following week.

SHOPS IN BORCHESTER: THEN

Daleys	Farm Implements
Jordans	Poulterers
Churchmans	Cooked meats
Harrisons	Ironmongers
Varley	Electrical Supplies
Merediths	Furniture
Jones and Croxley	Estate Agents and Auctioneers
Hoskins	Jewellers

Chapmans Toys	Toys
Martindales	Tailors
John Tregorran	Antiques/bookshop
Ann Prescott	Gown shop
Saddlers	Department Store
Bensons	Department Store (also in Felpersham)
Underwoods	Department Store
Rodway and Watson	Estate Agents and Auctioneers
Lockwoods	Gunsmiths
Wilsons	Car Accessories
Lennie's Discs	Boutique Records
Hodgetts	Garden shop
Gear Change	Fashion
Sidney's	Video Shop
Mathews	Drapers
Russell	Fish shop
Haskins	Bakers
Gerrards	Wine merchants
Nicole's	Sauna and massage
Hackfords	Carpet shop
Emery	Furniture shop

Half-day closing was on a Wednesday, except for Saddlers which, in an awkward or perhaps canny move, had its half-day closing on a Thursday.

TALES FROM THE GREENHOUSE

❧ The greenhouses at Grey Gables were where chauffeur-handyman-gardener Higgs raised Jack Woolley's prize-winning chrysanthemums for the Flower and Produce Show.

- In February 1998, Mike felled Marjorie Antrobus's beech tree – which fell straight onto her greenhouse. Neither was insured for such a calamity, so Mike's fee for the job went on a replacement greenhouse which he got from Tom Forrest.
- In November 2008, the greenhouse at The Lodge suffered the same fate when a branch of a mighty oak fell on it during a storm.
- Joe has often dreamed of having a greenhouse in which to raise tomatoes for the Flower and Produce Show, but for the moment has to manage with the lean-to.
- In the 1960s and 1970s, Jack Woolley owned a Garden Centre where Tom and Pru Forrest worked, selling all manner of garden goods including greenhouses.
- The extensive glasshouses at Manor Court, which used to be a market garden, have now disappeared.
- One of Jennifer's assignations during her affair with her ex-husband, Roger Travers-Macy, was in the glasshouses at the Felpersham Botanical Gardens, where she found the insistent Mynah bird irritating rather than amusing.
- Neither Bridge Farm nor Home Farm has gone into glasshouses for their salad crops or soft fruit – instead, they use polytunnels.
- Derek Fletcher (inevitably) has a greenhouse.

FINGERPOST FLAP

The Council doubtless thought they were doing Ambridge a favour when a shiny new metal sign was promised as a replacement for the old fingerpost flattened by Marjorie Antrobus's careless reversing. They hadn't accounted, though, for Lynda Snell's immediate establishment of HOOF (Hands Off Our Fingerpost). Interestingly, almost the sole voice for modernity was that of

Mark Hebden, who, less than six months later, was to die in a road accident (though admittedly not one caused by the lack of a retro-reflective sign). Ambridge kept its fingerpost: another thing for the tireless villagers to maintain, along with the old-style phone box, now a Tourist Information kiosk.

BROOKFIELD FARM

Dan Archer took over the tenancy from his father and bought the farm (then 100 acres) when the Estate was sold by Squire Lawson-Hope in 1954. Dan ran the farm with help from his son Phil and various farm workers (chiefly Simon Cooper and Ned Larkin) until he retired in 1970. Phil then ran the farm with help from his son David and workers Jethro Larkin, Neil Carter and herdsmen Mike Tucker and Graham Collard. David married student Ruth Pritchard who was doing a placement on the farm. Phil handed over to David and Ruth in 2001.

Brookfield was a traditional mixed farm with cattle, sheep, pigs and chickens and arable. It was only in 1951 that Dan reluctantly bought a tractor, selling one Shire horse and putting the other out to grass. After an outbreak of foot-and-mouth in 1956, he restocked with Friesians instead of Shorthorns, a daring move at the time. In the 1960s, Brookfield was part of a three-farm co-operative, and by the end of the decade Dan had acquired both the other farms, bringing Brookfield up to 435 acres. Throughout the 1970s and 1980s, Brookfield retained its dairy herd and lambing flock and also ran an intensive pig-rearing unit. Phil added to Brookfield's acreage with 30 acres of Meadow Farm, but the 55 acres of Willow Farm bought in 1983 were sold again to meet a large tax bill on Dan's death in 1986, along with 3 acres and some old barns for conversion into housing. Phil later bought back 7 acres of the ex-Willow Farm land and Brookfield now stands at 469 acres.

In the twenty-first century, Ruth and David have taken some radical decisions, contracting out their harvesting to Home Farm and moving first into Hereford beef, sold direct to the public, and more recently into pasture-based grazing as part of a more extensive approach (they are also in the HLS agri-environment scheme). They have also experimented with Brown Swiss genetics in the dairy herd. They still have a large lambing flock (325 ewes) but the hens which remain are chiefly a hobby for Jill.

BERT'S WINNING POEM ON TALENT NIGHT

'THE WETTEST EVER WEATHER'

Above the dark horizon,
The thunder clouds were piling,
Lightning split the sullen sky.
Only the ducks were smiling.
September soaked the sodden plough,
October turned still wetter.
My Freda said she'd emigrate
If it didn't get much better.

THE VILLAGE PUMP

It was divine retribution when a skidding lorry demolished the plaque which Joe Grundy had had put up on the site of the former village pump in 1974: it was Joe's lorry which had demolished the pump in the first place. The wily farmer had got out of paying for a replacement reproduction pump by persuading the Parish Council that the cost was too high, but councillors should have known that extracting a promise from him to pay for a memorial plaque would rebound on them. In the event, Joe's name appeared twice in large type on the plaque and he erected it without proper permission.

GREAT AMBRIDGE MYSTERIES
#1 'THE MYSTERY OF THE MISSING TEA MONEY'

The village was riveted in 1983 when the Over-60s' tea money went missing. Under interrogation by an impatient Detective Sergeant Barry, who couldn't believe he was actually investigating such a trivial crime, Walter cracked and admitted that on the fateful day he'd put a Dutch guilder in with his contribution. He reasoned that, unable to eat the biscuits owing to his diabetes, he was entitled to pay less. When Sid, cashing up in the pub, found a Dutch guilder in the till, all that night's drinkers – Tom, Walter, Nelson, Joe and Dan – fell under suspicion, but the investigation stalled. Dave Barry could see his promotion to Special Branch fading away as he wasted time on the fruitless investigation, when the money suddenly turned up at the bottom of… THE WRONG CADDY. It had been put in the caddy with the Queen and Prince Philip on the lid instead of the one which sported a giant panda, and some tea dumped on top of it. But no one ever confessed to coincidentally passing Sid a guilder in their beer money.

SSSI

Thanks to the Grundys' neglect ('conservation-awareness' according to Joe), a five-acre meadow at Grange Farm was designated an SSSI (Site of Special Scientific Interest) in 1988. Joe was quick to capitalise on the tourist potential (and to bank the Nature Conservancy Council's compensation payments) but, to the disgust of the visiting Ambridge Over-60s, knew little about the flowers and plants *and* had the temerity to charge them for their cups of tea. Oliver and Caroline are more caring custodians and will proudly show off the meadow's saxifrage, granny's apron and purple knapweed.

MOVIE MAGIC

Joe Grundy recalls seeing *Casablanca* at the Borchester Plaza but, in the 1950s, the Astoria Cinema was the place to go. Christine Archer saw *Tilly of Bloomsbury* there, while her brother Phil was a huge film fan, seeing *All About Eve*, starring Bette Davis, with Grace Fairbrother. He later took both girlfriend Grace and his poultry girl Jane Maxwell to see James Stewart in *No Highway*. Thirty years later, Phil must have suffered serious pangs when the Astoria became an Odeon. Nigel, proud owner of a gorilla suit, however, was thrilled when one of the first films they showed was *Tarzan*.

IRONSTONE IN AMBRIDGE

Take away the chocolate-box cottages and the village green and replace with... winding gear? Two-up, two-down terraces? It could all have been so different when, in 1951, a botched ploughing job revealed a seam of ironstone under a potential 100 acres of Ambridge. But even then the village knew how to see off a developer, especially one called (as this one was) Crawford. A trial excavation was sabotaged, drill bits stolen and rods chucked in the Am, and a public meeting descended into characteristic chaos. Finally, the main players gave up on the scheme, and Ambridge was saved from a future of whippets and chapel.

BEST-KEPT VILLAGE SABOTAGE!

Having made it to the nail-biting finals of the Best-Kept Village Competition in 1987 there was outrage when Ambridge came second to Loxley Barrett. Their comedown? A pile of beer cans in the village pond. It was sabotage, villagers were convinced, by the Loxley Barrett Morris Men – under cover of their performance at the village fete. Only three years later came another disaster – with the final judging days away, the pond this time threw up a human jawbone, complete with single tooth. It belonged to poor Florrie Hoskins who, pregnant and disgraced, had drowned herself there in 1905.

ALL ABOUT LOWER LOXLEY

From the Lower Loxley brochure

THE HOUSE

Largely constructed in 1702 on older foundations. Of especial interest to the visitor are the notable staircase, the ballroom and the Long Gallery with its fine paintings. Most of the house, apart from the conference rooms and family accommodation, is open to the public with regular tours by informative and friendly local guides. There is a Toy Museum in the old Nursery.

THE GROUNDS

- Cedric Pargetter's Victorian Folly
- Rupert Pargetter Memorial
- Tree Top Walk through the established Arboretum.
- Rare Breeds Farm – local ancient breeds of cattle, sheep, hens and pigs, housed in original buildings
- Heavy horse rides with Shire Horse Cranford Crystal and her cart
- Recently restored ha-ha
- Vineyard

A cycle route is marked around the grounds – a free map is available from the gift shop. Bike hire is available – or bring your own.

- Orangery Café serving hot meals, light snacks and drinks
- Gift shop
- Art Gallery – fine paintings by local artists

FIELD NAMES AT BRIDGE FARM

Bridge Close
Cowslip Meadow
Front Field
Big Leys
Long Meadow
Home Field
Six Acre
Kingcups
Primrose Bank
Far Pasture
Ashmead

Low Field
Top Field
The Dell
Tarbutts
The Hill

OCCUPANTS OF
ST STEPHEN'S GRAVEYARD

Laid to rest here are:

William and Lisa Forrest
Tom and Pru Forrest
John and Phoebe Archer
Grace Archer
Dan and Doris Archer
Laura Archer
John Archer
Lisa Scroby
'Granny' Watkins
Bill Slater
Amos 'Piggy' Atkins
Bob Larkin
Ned Larkin
Lizzie Larkin
Mabel Larkin
Jethro Larkin
Jess Allard
Susan Grundy
Zebedee Tring
Arthur Tovey
Agatha Turvey

Polly Perks
Ken Pound
Joby and Martha Woodford
Rose Blossom
Bill Insley
Walter and Nelson Gabriel
Polly Perkins (Mrs P)
Hubert Wiesner
(gunner of a German plane shot down on the outskirts of Ambridge)
Mark Hebden
George Barford
Marjorie Antrobus
NB The Lawson-Hope family are laid in
their family vault inside the church.

CABARET NIGHT AT THE BULL

Bert aimed to capitalise on his first Talent Night success at The Bull with a comic poem about Jethro Larkin's false teeth, but after objections from Clarrie about her dad's memory, changed the protagonist to Freda, and hers. On the night, up against a contortionist from Edgeley and 'Andy and his musical saw', Bert lost the script of his epic poem. As he attempted it from memory, heckling from Joe amused everyone except Bert. When the missing poem turned up in the pocket of Freda's overall, sabotage by the poem's subject was suspected, but Bert was mollified when she cooked him a slap-up meal with two bottles of Shires Export.

LOWER LOXLEY WINE

Nigel first had the idea of wine-making in 2003. Lizzie, tempted by the idea of sipping 'Chateau Loxley' on the terrace, immediately gave the idea her blessing and Nigel took advice from a grower called Vernon. As a result, Nigel decided on white grapes in two varieties – mainly Madeleine Angevine with some Seyval blanc. He started with 1,500 vines at £1.00 apiece, planting them on the south-facing slopes behind the Rare Breeds Centre and in the lee of the copses.

Nigel calculated that the potential markets for the wine would be the shop, the restaurant and Lower Loxley's conference trade. He also planned to put a bottle in the summer picnic and Christmas hampers which Lower Loxley supplies on request. A further market emerged when Lower Loxley started doing 'green' weddings, which use only local produce.

In 2006, pickers included Ruth, David, Sophie, Roy, Hayley, Phoebe, Shula, Alistair, Phil, Jill, Tom and Brenda. In that year, the wine could still not be sold, but pickers received a dozen bottles each as a thank you.

Nigel works with a winemaker called John Simons. After much agonising, he elected to go with a green glass Bordelaise-shape bottle with a cork rather than a screw top. The bottle caps are gold with two green stripes and after even more agonising, during which he rejected a more modern design, Nigel settled on a label with a simple line drawing of the house.

The wine has a dry feel, with a hint of new grass, though with no overpowering citrus note. The primary aromas are fairly complex, comprising hedgerow, nettles and elderflower, with a slight spritziness at the finish.

Nigel's efforts were rewarded in 2008, when Lower Loxley wine was finally accorded 'Regional Wine Status' under the full title of 'Lower Loxley Wine: an English regional wine from Borsetshire'.

There's a tasting display by the till in the shop and, encouragingly, over half the people who taste the wine buy at least one bottle. Elizabeth gives a twenty per cent discount to family and Jill took a couple of bottles to Sidmouth when she went to visit her friend Diana.

ICE-CREAM WARS

In 1984/5 Nigel and Elizabeth ran rival ice-cream vans. Nigel was between jobs and Elizabeth was still a student.

- Nigel was Mr Snowy

- Elizabeth was Ms Snowy

- Nigel's van played 'The Teddy Bears' Picnic'

- Elizabeth's van played 'Greensleeves'

- Pat was furious when both vans converged on the village green to tempt the children getting off the school bus

SHOPS IN BORCHESTER: NOW

Ambridge Organics	Organic produce
Morrison's	Jokes and Novelties
Bentham's	Ladies shoe shop
Sweet Celebrations	Specialist cake shop

Aladdin's cave	Antiques and second-hand jewellery
Dixon's	Pawnbrokers
Borsetshire Brides	Wedding shop
Gino's Deli, West St.	Makes good puddings and sells fresh pasta
Butcher	Canal Street
Supermarket	On the ring road

PUBS, RESTAURANTS AND CAFÉS

The Three Tuns	Live music on Tuesday nights
The Old Corn Mill	Down by the river, it used to be The Dirty Duck
The Blue Boar	A rough pub – too rough even for Jazzer's brother Stu!
The King's Head	A gay bar
The Goat and Nightgown	A large pub near the hospital
The Lord Kitchener	
Noah's Ark	A theme pub
Jaxx	Kenton's cafe
El Dorado	A tapas bar in Abbey St.

TAKE IT AWAY

A selection of light music from the Grey Gables Restaurant
in the 1950s – played by the Queen's Hall Light Orchestra:

'By the Stream'
'Buffoon'
'Serenade' (from the Joyous Youth Suite)
'Tête-à-tête'
'Holiday Spirit'
'Willie the Whistler'

SEEING THE FUNNY SIDE

In October 2002, Elizabeth was disconcerted when, about to welcome a party of bank managers for a conference, she observed them laughing and pointing at something outside in the grounds. Three pairs of her knickers had been run up the Lower Loxley flagpole with the legend 'N ♥ E' on them, the result of a night's revelry involving Nigel, Kenton, Alistair and Brookfield worker Chaba. Elizabeth's wasn't the only red face: when Alistair, on a routine veterinary call, asked Debbie to pass him something from his bag, she produced a pair of black lacy knickers, planted there by the others.

SEVEN LOCAL MEMORIALS

- The Lawson-Hope seat (on the Green)
- The Dan Archer Memorial Playground
- John Archer's tree (in the churchyard)
- Greg Turner's tree (in the woods)
- Betty Tucker's apple tree (in the garden at Willow Farm)
- George Barford's bridge over the Am
- Siobhan Hathaway's bench and table, and 'mummy's tree' (according to Ruairi) in the Millennium Wood

AMBRIDGE CALLING

Shula has happy memories of the village phone box (now a mini-Tourist Information Centre). She once phoned Jill from it as soon as she got off the school bus to announce she'd won the cross country at school and also used it for presumably secret, if not illicit, calls to an old boyfriend,

Steve Cartwright. When British Telecom threatened to replace it with a new-style vandal-proof booth in 1990, she led the campaign to save it. Martha Woodford used to clean the box and garland it with hanging baskets in summer and Christmas decorations in winter. When Martha died, Marjorie Antrobus took over her cleaning duties.

BROKEN STRINGS

At a Bull talent contest in 1977, the winners were
a group called The Wild Spots. Shula's guitar string broke
but she still got a special mention.

GRANGE FARM

The Grundys were tenants – and not particularly good ones – at Grange Farm until forced out by bankruptcy in 2000. The house and 50 acres were bought by hobby farmer Oliver Sterling, the rest of the land being absorbed back into the Estate. Initially stocking the farm with beef cattle, Oliver managed these with the help of Ed Grundy, in whom he took a paternal interest. A growing interest in local produce led Oliver to sell the beef cattle and invest in a small herd of Guernseys, establishing a milk round with the help of Ed and local milkman Mike Tucker's existing contacts. This prospered and, using Helen Archer's expertise, the Guernsey milk also went to make a semi-hard cheese named Sterling Gold. After TB struck the herd in 2008, however, Oliver seemed tempted to give it all up, but his close relationship with Ed offered a way forward. While Oliver concentrates his efforts more at Grey Gables, the country house hotel he co-owns with his wife Caroline, his generous terms have enabled Ed to become the tenant farmer at Grange Farm. To the Grundy family's delight, the wheel has come full circle.

BATS BATTLED

Bats are a protected species, so when Phil found bat droppings on the church organ in 1996, Tom Forrest employed some devious methods to try to move them on:

- Getting John Archer to play organ music through his disco equipment
- Putting a stuffed owl behind the pulpit to act as 'scarecrow'
- Hanging mothballs in the gallery
- A dog whistle, which only upset Nelson's dog Charlie

The bats did move on but returned the following year, when they were seen flying around Ambridge Hall.

REGULAR
(AND NOT-SO-REGULAR)
EVENTS AT GREY GABLES

Cookery evenings and demonstrations
Murder Mystery Weekend
May Ball
New Year's Eve Ball
Valentine's Ball
Fashion Shows
Jitterbug Ball – for the Anniversary of D-Day
One-day Creative Writing Course (taught by Jennifer)
Tea Dances
Docu-soap made about the hotel

IN THE TOY MUSEUM
AT LOWER LOXLEY

At least three teddy bears:
Growler (1910)
Monty
Tiddles (Nigel's favourite)
Mickey Monkey
Dobbin the rocking horse
Punch and Judy theatre and puppets
Dolls
Toy soldiers

DISHES FROM
THE HASSETT ROOM

In 1995, Kathy Perks, a former Home Economics teacher, had the idea to turn The Bull's restaurant into one with a Civil War theme. She did extensive research into authentic recipes, but the eventual menu raised eyebrows among the regulars – and that was before they'd even tasted the food. Featured on the menu were:

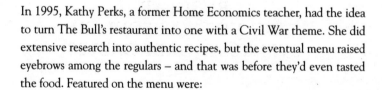

- Salamagundy
- Syllabub
- Roast saddle of mutton
- Humble Pie
- Cromwell Pudding

The chef was Owen King (aka Gareth Taylor), and Susan was a waitress. The restaurant lasted barely two years – from May 1995 to June 1997.

FIELD NAMES AT HOME FARM

Long Field (by Long Wood)
Long Meadow
White Acre
Broad Bank
Broad Field
Top Field
Oak Bank
High Copse
Lakefield (on the left past Ambridge Hall)

WHAT'S AROUND AMBRIDGE?

- Pumping station
- Romano-British site
- Two gravel pits (disused)
- Site of medieval village (near Grange Farm)
- Medieval settlement (remains)
- Tumuli (on Lakey Hill)
- Burial mound (Heydon Rise)
- Electricity sub-station
- Water treatment works
- Three allotments
- Barn conversions
- A small pond
- A milestone indicating distance to Borchester

BED AND BREAKDOWN

In 1993, Phil and Jill went to Australia to visit Kenton, leaving the
rest of the family (Ruth, David, Shula and Mark) to cope with the
Brookfield B&B. They endured the guests from hell…

THE WHEELERS

Vegetarians. Mr Wheeler fancied himself as a bit of a wit, shouting,
'Oi, Manuel' every time he saw Mark at breakfast.

THE BARTLETTS

Had a brat of a child who demanded Coco Pops every day except
Wednesdays, when he wanted Sugar Puffs.

THE LITTLEJOHNS

Mr Littlejohn was allergic to gluten and also had problems with
polyester, which brought him out in a rash. Shula forgot and
gave him polyester sheets when she changed the beds.

JOLENE'S MONEYSPINNERS
AT THE BULL

- Quiz Nite
- Curry Night
- Midweek Carvery
- Darts matches
- Cybercafe

Plus:
- Function Room 'The Bull Upstairs' with special music nights
- Mulled wine and mince pies for the Christmas Lights Switch-On

- Bonfire Night – Punch
- 'Pigs in blankets' – sausages in baked potatoes
- Vegetarian chilli
- Toffee apples and cinder toffee
- BBQ/Pork Roast and drinks, plus running of beer tent, on Fete Day
- Easter Egg Hunt/Egg Rolling/Easter Bonnet Competition

GREAT AMBRIDGE MYSTERIES
#2 'THE MYSTERY OF THE MAIL VAN ROBBERY'

When Nelson Gabriel died in 2001, former Ambridge PC (by now a Detective Inspector) Jim Coverdale had to come back for the funeral – to make sure the old smoothie and law-bender, if not breaker, was actually dead. The nearest Nelson ever came to a conviction was for the Borchester Mail Van Robbery in 1967, but his fingerprints on a whisky bottle at the crooks' hideout were judged circumstantial. Fifteen years later, the police couldn't make a charge of masterminding an antiques ring stick either and his loyal dad Walter maintained stoutly that Nelson had been picked on by the police ever since he was a boy. Odd that Nelson ended up in South America, for so long a haven for known offenders.

PLANES

- Brian had flying lessons in the early 1980s. When he took Jennifer up to photograph the deserted medieval village of Ambridge she felt sick.
- A jet plane crashed into Dan's Five Acre Field in August 1952, spoiling an excellent crop of wheat.
- When an RAF trainer plane crashed near Heydon Berrow

in 1972, the pilot had to bale out. He landed in the sewage farm near Borchester.

- During the Second World War, the Borchester anti-aircraft gun shot down a German plane which crashed on Grange Farm land near the Am.

- When a lump of the wreckage was exposed in 1995, the gunner's body was found to be still in the cockpit. He was buried in St Stephen's churchyard.

- Alice is studying Aeronautical Engineering at Southampton University. She failed to gain sponsorship from the RAF – she passed the first set of interviews but not the second.

- In 2004, Kenton bought Jill a microlight flight as a gift. Jill so enjoyed the half-hour experience that she even briefly took over the controls.

- When working as a commercial pilot, Lilian's boyfriend Lester Nicholson went missing in the Brazilian jungle.

- One of the ill-fated business efforts of Christine's first husband Paul Johnson was a crop-spraying venture in East Anglia.

- David Archer owns a remote-controlled plane but doesn't have much time to fly it.

FIELD NAMES AT BROOKFIELD

The Grove	Trefoil	Little Field
Midsummer Meadow	The Croft	Upper Parks
Lower Parks	Long Field	Wormitts
Burntland	Lakey Meadow	Badger's Bank
Skipperley	Round Robin	Ashfield
Marney's	Lakey Hill	Coombebell
Blacklands	Oakey Bank	

A WHEEL AT EACH CORNER...

- Eddie's pride and joy in the 1980s was his Ford Capri with furry dice dangling from the mirror. He now owns a van with the inscription 'Eddie's Garden Products – Landscape Gardener, Garden Makeovers', and an illustration of one of his ornaments – a cheeky pig.
- In 1989, Brian bought a new Mercedes with a tracking device.
- In a mini crime wave in 1999, Mr Booth's car was stolen while he was at bell-ringing practice. It was found miles away, a burnt-out wreck.
- Phil was once knocked off the running board of Grace Fairbrother's car by an overhanging branch. He had leapt onto it to try to reason with her during one of their not infrequent tiffs.
- Brookfield has a Land Rover and Home Farm a Range Rover.
- As well as Tom's pride, another casualty of his failed supermarket deal was his prized new Mini Cooper. He had to sell it and get a cheaper, older car.
- In the brat pack of the 1980s, Borsetshire 'IT' girl Jackie Woodstock drove a white Triumph Spitfire and David a red one, while Nigel's friend Tim Beecham wowed the ladies in a blue Austin-Healey Sprite.
- Kenton has a 4x4 off-road vehicle. The local off-roaders club is run by Jason, the Brummie builder.
- When Ruth's mum got a new car, Ruth inherited Heather's old Mini Metro.
- Vet-cum-vicar Robin Stokes drove a Volvo estate.
- Mrs Antrobus had a 'half-timbered' Morris Minor Traveller.
- For her 21st birthday, Debbie's estranged father, Roger Travers-Macy, presented her with a Golf GTI.
- Jack Woolley's chauffeur/handyman, Higgs, was the proud custodian of Jack's Bentley.
- In his tearaway days, Sid used to have a souped-up Ford Zodiac.
- As well as renovating a Fordson tractor, Tony stripped and reconditioned an old MG, his pride and joy.
- Seeing Tony's car prompted Alistair's father, Jim, to buy a classic car.

Having wavered between an MG and a Triumph Herald, he finally settled on a Riley.

20 SERVICES IN BORCHESTER

1. The District Council buildings are in Parliament Road near the college.
2. A local builder is (Don) Cullinford Construction, off Rowland Road, Borchester.
3. Borchester Leisure Centre has a soft play area.
4. Borchester is twinned with a German town – Rhona is the local organiser.
5. Tilbury Street is in the rough part of Borchester.
6. There is a night club called 'Pearly Gates' on Tilbury Street.
7. The Elms Centre for the homeless is in Borchester.
8. There's a bowling alley – Susan knows someone who works there.
9. Borchester has a Poodle Parlour.
10. Borsetshire Gamekeepers Association is based there.
11. There are loft-style apartments by the canning factory.
12. The farm suppliers are called Borsetshire Farmers.
13. Concerts are given by Felpersham Choral Society in Borchester Town Hall – the acoustics are not the best in the world but with a big choir it can sound impressive.
14. There is a bandstand in Borchester Park which has graffiti on it.
15. There's a garden centre on the way to Borchester.
16. A regular bus leaves Borchester early on Wednesday mornings but it goes via Layton Cross, Perivale, St John's and Rosserran down through Darrington and on to Ambridge: it takes a very long time.
17. Borchester Register Office is lacking in atmosphere.
18. There is a Multiplex cinema.
19. Borchester Town Hall has the 'Rippon Suite'.
20. All Saints Church is in Borchester.

THE BULL

Jack and Peggy Archer bought the freehold of Ambridge's local in 1959. They'd previously run it for the Borchester Brewery (1951–1957), then the Stourhampton Brewery (1957–1959). The asking price of £5,300 seemed like an astronomical sum at the time and they only managed it with the help of a £4,000 interest-free loan from the eccentric and wealthy Aunt Laura. But it proved a shrewd investment. When Peggy sold it in 1993, the pub was valued at £250,000 and, by the time of Sid and Kathy Perks's divorce in 2001, The Bull's estimated worth was £300,000. Sid and Jolene Perks are now co-owners with Lilian Bellamy.

The beer is now the ever-popular Shires, though Sid occasionally offers guest beers from the new microbreweries. The Bull serves bar snacks and full meals in the family restaurant, all 'home-cooked' by Freda Fry.

There are two bars, the public bar and the posher Ploughman's. Bar staff in addition to Sid and Jolene include Kirsty Miller, who also works at Ambridge Organics, Clarrie, who also works at Pat's dairy, and Jolene's daughter Fallon, doing her best to hide her disappointment at the fact that her musical career has not yet taken off.

Over the years, The Bull has also been home to:

- The Playbar – a coffee/milk bar to attract 'a younger crowd'
- A steak bar
- Nouvelle cuisine, introduced by Kathy Perks
- A Civil War themed Restaurant, 'The Hassett Room'
- And now the reliable Family Room restaurant

BRIDGE FARM

Pat and Tony were long-time tenants of the Bellamy (also known as Berrow) Estate, meaning that Tony's sister was also his landlord. In 1984, they'd been having a tough time personally and were facing the imposition of milk quotas when Tony had a Damascene conversion and, with Pat's full approval, converted the farm to organic production. Pat's help was vital as their first task was to add value to their milk, which is turned into a successful range of yogurt, cream and ice cream. Tony manages the dairy herd and oversees the smallish cereal acreage but much of his time is taken up with the labour-intensive vegetable crops (potatoes, cabbage, leeks and root crops) and salads which are grown in polytunnels. These are sold through their Borchester shop, Ambridge Organics and Wholefoods, which is run by their daughter Helen. She also uses their milk to make Borsetshire Blue cheese.

In 2008, Helen and her brother Tom were united in pushing their parents to buy the freehold of the 140-acre farm and secure their future. This Pat and Tony have done (with a large mortgage) and Tom has set up an organic pig herd which will go to make the sausages for which he is famous.

A FINE VINTAGE

Lower Loxley wine is not the first in the locality. Carol and John Tregorran used to produce Manor Court wine in the 1970s.

CARAVAN OF LOVE

In the 1970s, a struggling Pat and Tony thought a caravan site might boost their income but it only lasted a couple of years.

One of the remaining caravans, though, later came in useful for single mother Sharon, Pat's dairy worker, who briefly lived there with her daughter Kylie before getting a council house. Pat and Tony's elder son John proved the strength of his feelings for Sharon when he emptied her chemical toilet.

In 1995, Tony himself had to take refuge in the caravan when Pat accused him of having an affair with a girl called Sandy, though Sandy's real interest was in the Fordson tractor Tony was restoring.

TROUBLE AT THE TOWER

In the 1950s, Walter Gabriel, Simon Cooper, Tom Forrest, Dan, Phil and even the flighty Jack Archer were the stalwarts of the bell-ringing team, but when their special peal for the Coronation in 1953 wasn't up to his exacting standards, Tom blamed Walter and demanded they shape up. Walter blamed his performance on the new sally, saying he preferred a worn one every time. As Tom tutted, Dan revealed that he had once been lifted ten feet off the floor because he wasn't handling his bell right – though, in fairness, he was only 10 years old at the time.

IN A HOLIDAY MOOD

Never let it be said that the villagers of Ambridge have horizons stretching only as far as Borchester. In the early 1960s, when 'abroad' was still viewed with some trepidation and package holidays were in their infancy, the Archers and friends were intrepid travellers.

Dan and Doris to Guernsey, 20 Sept–2 Oct 1963
Phil, Jill and the children to Newquay, end of July 1964
Dan and Doris to Malaga with Fred and Betty Barratt, 2–16 Oct 1964
Carol Grenville, Richard and the nanny to St Just in Roseland,
beginning of Sept 1965
Dan and Doris, Fred and Betty to Ireland, end of Sept 1965
Jack and Peggy to the Italian Riviera, first two weeks in May 1966
Dan and Doris, Sid and Polly to Scotland, 28 Aug–11 Sept 1967
Jack and Peggy, Fred and Betty Barratt – a cruise, 1967
Phil, Jill and the children to the Isle of Man, 1968

REGULAR EVENTS THROUGHOUT THE YEAR AT LOWER LOXLEY

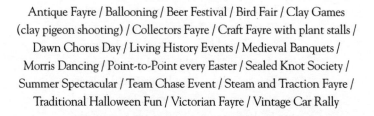

Antique Fayre / Ballooning / Beer Festival / Bird Fair / Clay Games
(clay pigeon shooting) / Collectors Fayre / Craft Fayre with plant stalls /
Dawn Chorus Day / Living History Events / Medieval Banquets /
Morris Dancing / Point-to-Point every Easter / Sealed Knot Society /
Summer Spectacular / Team Chase Event / Steam and Traction Fayre /
Traditional Halloween Fun / Victorian Fayre / Vintage Car Rally

Lower Loxley also offers Falconry Courses and Schools Visits as well as weddings ('green' weddings a speciality), conference and corporate bookings, and Christmas packages.

THE BULL'S NETTLE-EATING COMPETITION (2003)

Entrants included:

Mike

David

Jazzer

Roy

Tom

Bert

Nigel

Kenton

Kirsty

Nathan Booth

Mike Tucker had heard of a similar event in Dorset and suggested the idea as an attraction for The Bull. The nettles were to be cut in two-foot lengths and contestants had to strip off the leaves (no gloves allowed), fold them up, chew and swallow them down with a swig of beer.

When Eddie saw Jazzer practising by munching handfuls of nettles in the churchyard, he thought he'd spotted a sure-fire winner. Eddie promptly opened a book on the event and, to distract attention from Jazzer's prowess, he and Joe put word round the village that Mike was the favourite. Adam put £10 on Mike, whose secret was thought to be his calloused hands which would withstand any amount of nettle stings.

On the day:

🗲 Kirsty was eliminated when Eccles the peacock stole her nettles

- Jazzer, suffering toothache, dropped out – to Eddie's dismay
- Roy kept getting stung
- Tom didn't turn up
- David conceded to Mike
- Nathan Booth was disqualified for having ice cubes in his pocket to numb his mouth
- Mike was about to declare at four lengths when Bert was seen to be still steadily munching away
- Bert was declared winner at five lengths

HAPPY HONEYMOONS

Honeymoon destinations have included:

Christine and George	Tunisia
Jack and Peggy Woolley	The Caribbean
Marjorie and Teddy	The White Sands Hotel, Kilifi, Kenya
Phil and Jill	Touring England, ending up in London
Shula and Mark	Fishing on the Tweed, Scotland
Shula and Alistair	St Kitts and Nevis, Caribbean
David and Ruth	A week in Lanzarote
Nigel and Elizabeth	Bali
Jennifer and Roger	A weekend in London then a week in Ibiza with Adam
Jennifer and Brian	Touring farming country near Cambridge
Debbie and Simon	Paris
Lilian and Ralph	Venice
Pat and Tony	Tenerife

Eddie and Clarrie	Torremolinos
Bert and Freda	Llandudno – it rained
Susan and Neil	A guesthouse in Cornwall
Roy and Hayley	A long weekend in London
Will and Emma	Cancun, Mexico then Great Yarmouth to see Clarrie's sister
Caroline and Robin	Venice (planned but wedding cancelled)
Caroline and Guy	A small hotel in the foothills of the Pyrenees
Caroline and Oliver	Perth Game Fair; then later in the year, St Lucia
Sid and Polly	Devon and Cornwall
Sid and Kathy	The Lake District
Sid and Jolene	Nashville
Adam and Ian	Kenya – Adam used to work there
Alan and Usha	A night in London; Eurostar to Paris then on to Rome, ending up in the Italian Lakes
Mike and Vicky	A week on the Isle of Wight; then an immediate 'second honeymoon' in Brittany (not quite the Caribbean cruise Vicky had imagined)

SID'S AMBITIONS

After The Bull won 'South Borsetshire Pub of the Year' in 2004, Sid went all out for the wider 'Borsetshire Pub of the Year' in 2005. 'Improvements' included a new menu, though sadly the hoped-for refinements were lost on the pub's cook, Freda Fry.

Bar Menu

Steak and Kidney Pie **OFF**
Chicken and Mushroom Pie **OFF**
Chicken and Leek Pie **OFF**

Margherita Pizza **OFF**
Ham and Mushroom Pizza **OFF**
Four Seasons Pizza **OFF**

TRY OUR *NEW SEAFOOD MENU!!!*
Shrimp Tagliatelli
Baked Salmon
(with Tomato Ketchup or Tartare Sauce 50p extra)

OR A *HEALTHY SALAD*
Caesar Salad
(with Salad Cream or Pickle 50p extra)

TRY OUR *SELECTION OF FINE WINES OR
NEW! LOCAL MINERAL WATER*

PLEASE NOTE:
NO OVERALLS OR WELLIES IN THE BAR

HOME FARM

Home Farm was created from the sale of parts of the Bellamy Estate in the mid 1970s. Brian Aldridge, who'd sold his Hertfordshire farm for development, bought the house and 1,500 acres and, for the next 25 years, ran it pretty aggressively as an agri-business, though diversification grants in the 1990s tempted him into opening a riding course and fishing lake. Brian is now semi-retired. The running of the farm is divided between Adam, who does the day-to-day arable management and oversees the livestock (sheep and deer) and his own enterprise (soft fruit) and Debbie, who has a more strategic role in things like cropping plans. She works from Hungary, also overseeing Brian's farming interests there. In addition, she works for the Estate, which is now owned by Borchester Land, a company chaired by Brian.

Home Farm, now 1,585 acres thanks to the acquisition of two parcels of land which were formerly Willow Farm, has a large cereal acreage but has recently dropped its second lambing flock, leaving Adam with just 280 ewes to lamb in January. The riding course and fishing lake remain, but another diversification, a maize maze, proved more trouble than it was worth.

COURT IN THE ACT

When Phil was a JP in the late 1980s, three of his fellow magistrates were Mr Morris, Major Bigsby and the formidable Myra Prestwick, with whom Phil became somewhat besotted. The Borchester Courts had loomed large from the beginning: at the Petty Sessions in 1953, George Fairbrother and Dan were accused by Ben White of shooting his pigeons. Fairbrother was fined 10/- with 8 guineas costs; Dan's case was dismissed. In 1983, there was something of Hobson's choice when Ben Warner, a drifter whom Shula had befriended, was tried for burglary. Depending on the time of day, he could have got lucky with Judge Hiscox who was very fond of port, but Ben got Judge Banks ('Bloody Banks') who sent him down for 12 months.

PARKING ROOM

In 1977 (not 1877) Borchester still had an Assembly Rooms, though not for much longer. By the end of the year they had been torn down – to be replaced with a multi-storey car park.

AMAZING MAIZE

Designs for the Home Farm maze have included:
- The Magi-maze – Harry Potter theme (a wizard shape)
- The Alien maze – a spaceship design – slogan: 'Out Of This World'
- Bad weather meant the maize did not grow to sufficient height for the maze to open
- The Dino-maze – a dinosaur design – slogan 'Come and Have a Mammoth Experience'

In 2009, Adam dropped the maze after the disappointment of two rainy summers.

FELPERSHAM
THROUGH THE YEARS

These facts were recorded about Felpersham in 1951:
- 16 miles from Ambridge but only ten miles on the direct road from Borchester

- Population 20,000
- It had an Isolation Hospital: Tel: Felpersham 2358
- And an Infirmary: Tel Felpersham 2184 (Visiting days Thursday – Sunday; Eye specialist Dr Harvey)
- The *Felpersham Gazette* was published on Fridays

Felpersham was also home to:

- George Fairbrother's plastics factory, which sent items to the South Bank Exhibition of the Festival of Britain
- Shops included Grainger's (a dress shop) and Thomas and Riley (a department store)
- There was a Brock's Hotel
- It used to have a ginger beer brewery, William Dudley and Sons

By the 1980s Felpersham could claim:

- A Country and Western Club
- A prison
- A cathedral with bookstall and café
- A racecourse
- A theatre
- A careers office
- Bethal's the antique shop
- Benson's department store
- Mitchell's the builder's merchants
- An organic store selling Pat Archer's yogurt
- A dry ski slope
- A good coffee centre, used by Jennifer
- Botanical Gardens
- A Country Park

GREAT AMBRIDGE MYSTERIES
#3 'THE MYSTERY OF THE SPEEDING CAR'

When Mark Hebden died at the wheel of his car in 1994, leaving Caroline in a coma and a pole-axed Shula pregnant with Daniel (a fact Mark never knew), the greatest mystery was not and has never been solved. Who was driving the speeding car which overtook Mark on a blind bend, scaring Caroline's horse, throwing her into the road and making Mark crash into a tree to avoid her? The police investigation went nowhere but, if it wasn't a random stranger, the smart money has always been on Guy Pemberton's son Simon. It would be easy to believe he could have been a dangerous driver. He later romanced Shula before showing his vicious side and leaving the village under a cloud.

MOBILE LIBRARY

In 1982, the mobile library called in Ambridge every other Friday (calling at Penny Hassett on the alternate weeks). Its stopping times were:

11.30 – 12.00	Close to The Green (council houses)
12.00 – 1.00	Other side of Village Green, near the shop
1.00 – 2.00	The librarian always had his lunch in The Bull

Before and after these times, the van called at outlying areas around the village, stopping for no more than ten minutes in each place. The van carried 2,500 books but, strangely, none were for children.

OTHER FARMS
AROUND AMBRIDGE

- Two Bank Farms
- Bull Farm House (home of Charles and Jean Harvey)
- Green Farm
- Heydon Farm
- Meadow Farm
- Overton Farm
- Red House Farm
- Sawyers Farm (housing the Estate Office and the Business Units)
- Valley Farm